AMERICA

Celebrates

COLUMBUS

Credits

Profits from the sale of this cookbook are used to support community projects of the Junior League of Columbus, Inc.

The Junior League of Columbus is an organization of women committed to promoting voluntarism, developing the potential of women, and improving communities through the effective action and leadership of trained volunteers. Its purpose is exclusively educational and charitable.

America Celebrates Columbus is the companion book to the successful *America Discovers Columbus* cookbook presented by the Junior League of Columbus.

America Celebrates Columbus has been created from the excellent recipes contributed by Junior League of Columbus members, their families, and friends. Every recipe was tested, retested, then tested again. We invite you to celebrate the rich tradition of the heartland in this culinary tour of Columbus, the crossroads of America. Please share in and enjoy this bountiful harvest of sophisticated but easy-to-prepare recipes.

America Celebrates Columbus
Copyright © 1999 by
The Junior League of Columbus, Inc.
583 Franklin Avenue
Columbus, Ohio 43215-4715
614-470-2955

The Junior League of Columbus would like to recognize and thank **Borders Books, Music & Cafe** for their support of *America Celebrates Columbus*.

Edited, Designed, and Manufactured by Favorite Recipes® Press an imprint of

P.O. Box 305142
Nashville, Tennessee 37230
800-358-0560

Designer: Jim Scott
Book Project Manager: Linda A. Jones

Manufactured in the United States of America
First Printing: 1999 10,000 copies

Library of Congress Catalog Number: 99-071710
ISBN: 0-9613621-1-1

Artwork by Erin Kelly Murphy

(FRONT COVER ARTWORK: *Front View of the Kelton House* **/ BACK COVER ARTWORK:** *Rear View of the Kelton House*)

Acknowledgements

Special Appreciation to the following League members who gave countless hours, invaluable advice, and support. Your efforts made *America Celebrates Columbus* possible. Thank you!

Wanda Anderson
Jenny Lynn Baber
Marci Biel
Rebecca Bugos
Donna Vuletic Caldwell
Mary Campbell
Melinda Carlson
Trish Colby
Miranda Cox
Valorie Whiston Crusey
Mary Cusick
Lynne Deshler
Mary Dorsey
Nancy Drees
Amy Dunn
Beth Eck
JoAnn Fehring
Susan Fortner
J-Anna Fry
Jill Joslin Gilbert
Janie Greiner
Jill Guth
Wendy Haddow
Katherine C. Hamilton
Erin Hampton
Carol Hawks
Lisa Hays
Robin Hepler
Ronda Hobart

Alice Hood
Kathy Houck
Kelley Hughes
Sarah Irvin
Lynne Jeffrey
Liza Jupinko
Cynthia Karkut
Susan Keferl
Lori Kimm
Suzanne Kull
Suzy Lhamon
Trish Looby
Jean Lavoie
Suzy Kramer Lucci
Kara Manchester
Dawn Marable
Linda McDonald
Rebecca McNemar
Sally Meier
Stephanie Midkiff
Lynette Mock-Sherman
Erin Murphy
Renee Nicholson
Annita Paolucci
Sue Pinkerton
Nicole Evans Porter
Nancy Prellwitz
Sue Rakowich
Cortney Randall

Susan Rector
Amy Rhoades
Margie Van Meter Rolf
Lynda Schockman
Lynn Schwarz
Sheila Serrao
Marlee Snowdon
Catherine Talda
Peggy Tidwell
Amanda Trueman
Cathy Von Volkenburg
Dawn Wilcox
Mary Williams
Teresa Woodard
Hannah Yuhas

We sincerely hope that no one involved with this cookbook has been inadvertently overlooked.

Table of Contents

INTRODUCTION   6

TEATIME AT THE KELTON HOUSE MUSEUM AND GARDEN   8
Menu: An Afternoon Invitation

CELEBRATED BEGINNINGS   28
Menu: A Work of Art

SALADS AND SOUPS   44
Menu: Let's Do Lunch

ENTRÉES   62
Menu: An Enchanted Evening

PASTA   88
Menu: A Special Gathering

SIDE DISHES 104

Menu: The Game Plan

BRUNCH AND BREADS 120

Menu: Blue Ribbon Brunch

CELEBRATED ENDINGS 136

Menu: Sweet Dreams

CONTRIBUTORS 168

INDEX 170

ORDER INFORMATION 176

Introduction

Welcome to *America Celebrates Columbus.* The members of the Junior League of Columbus are thrilled to present the sequel to their successful first cookbook, *America Discovers Columbus.* For seventy-five years the members of the Junior League of Columbus have dedicated themselves to promoting voluntarism, developing the potential of women, and improving the community through the effective action and leadership of trained volunteers. It is our mission.

Trained volunteers are the Junior League's legacy to the community. One of the ways we train volunteers and contribute to the community is through our projects. The Junior League of Columbus was the genesis of many projects that now stand on their own and continue to serve the community. Examples include the Columbus Landmarks Foundation, OWjL, C.A.S.A. (Court Appointed Special Advocates), Community Information and Referral System, Inc. (a predecessor to FIRSTLINK), Columbus Junior Theater, and Artists in the Schools.

Throughout its history, the members of the Junior League of Columbus have striven to improve the lives of children. The Junior League established a Children's Mental Health Center (contributing $73,000 from 1949 to 1959), traveled to the schools as the Columbus Junior Theater, and provided funds, programs, and volunteers for the Faith Mission at the Make Room Columbus Family Center (contributing $26,000 in 1992). The current focus area of the Junior League of Columbus is middle school children. JUMP (Junior League Mentoring Project), the signature project of the Junior League of Columbus going into the next century, encourages middle school girls to take an active role in improving their community and helps them to develop the leadership skills necessary to do so. The Junior League of Columbus continues to support OWjL, a residential summer camp for gifted middle school students created by the Junior League and Ohio Wesleyan University.

Members of the Junior League of Columbus changed the face of this community. When Junior League volunteers started the gift shop at the Franklin Park Conservatory, a renewed interest developed and led to the renovation of the Conservatory. As part of its commitment to neighborhood revitalization, the Junior League of Columbus facilitated and funded the Town-Franklin Neighborhood Project, developing suggested guidelines for this downtown neighborhood with the Ohio State University Department of Architecture. The Kelton House Museum and Garden, a Victorian house restored by the Junior League as a decorative arts museum is featured in this book. The Junior League of Columbus also conducted a comprehensive survey of the arts community, published the results, and in the process organized the Columbus Arts' Council, the predecessor to the Greater Columbus Arts' Council.

The Junior League also provided significant funding to various nonprofit organizations. For example, the Junior League gave $16,000 in 1963 to COSI for the purchase of the Transparent Talking Woman; $8,500 in 1986 to the Afro-American Museum Education Outreach Project for the development and implementation of curriculum based on the opening exhibit for the National Afro-American Museum; and $23,700 in 1987 to Women and Widowhood to stabilize and expand career development services available at the Center for New Directions.

Thank you for supporting the community service projects of the Junior League of Columbus through the purchase of *America Celebrates Columbus*. Happy cooking and happy celebrating!

Teatime
at the Kelton House
Museum and Garden

AN AFTERNOON INVITATION

MENU

CHÈVRE AND HERB BUTTER TEA SANDWICHES – PAGE 10

CHIVE PUFFS WITH CURRIED CHICKEN FILLING – PAGE 14

COCONUT SCONES WITH AMERICAN DEVONSHIRE CREAM – PAGES 18 & 19

MINIATURE CHOCOLATE CHEESECAKES – PAGE 20

WELSH CHEESECAKES – PAGE 20

KELTON HOUSE
MUSEUM AND GARDEN

By pursuing the goals of education and preservation, the Junior League of Columbus realized the dream of Grace Kelton, who, in 1975, left her family home in trust to the Columbus Foundation. The Junior League stepped forward and adopted the Kelton House as its signature project. The Museum provides unique and realistic views into the past; a stop on the Underground Railroad, original furnishings and family records, and educational tours and programs. The Kelton House is located on East Town Street in the Discovery District.

Chèvre and Herb Butter Tea Sandwiches

YIELD: 16 SERVINGS

1/2 cup unsalted butter, softened
4 ounces cream cheese, softened
2 ounces chèvre or goat cheese, softened
1/2 cup chopped fresh parsley
1/2 cup chopped fresh basil

1/2 cup chopped fresh rosemary
Salt and freshly ground pepper to taste
16 thin slices firm wheat or oatmeal bread, crusts trimmed

PROCESS the butter, cream cheese, chèvre, parsley, basil and rosemary in a food processor until well blended. SEASON with salt and pepper. SPREAD over half the bread slices. TOP with the remaining bread slices. CUT into rectangles or triangles.

Cucumber and Mint Tea Sandwiches

YIELD: 12 SERVINGS

1/4 cup unsalted butter, softened
2 tablespoons finely chopped fresh mint

12 thin slices white bread, crusts trimmed
1/2 hothouse cucumber, peeled, sliced

COMBINE the butter and mint in a small bowl and mix well. SPREAD on each of the bread slices. ARRANGE the cucumber slices on the buttered side of half the bread slices. PLACE the remaining bread slices buttered side down on top of the cucumbers. CUT into rectangles or triangles.

Egg and Watercress Tea Sandwiches

YIELD: 12 SERVINGS

4 hard-cooked eggs
1 bunch watercress
1/4 cup (about) mayonnaise
Salt and freshly ground pepper
   to taste

12 thin slices firm white or oatmeal
   bread, crusts trimmed
1/4 cup unsalted butter, softened

PEEL the eggs and cut into quarters. RINSE the watercress and discard the center stems; drain. COMBINE the eggs and watercress in a food processor container. ADD enough of the mayonnaise gradually, processing constantly until of a spreadable consistency. SEASON with salt and pepper. SPREAD 1/2 of the bread slices with the butter. SPREAD the egg mixture over the butter. TOP with the remaining bread slices. CUT into rectangles or triangles.

Onion Tea Sandwiches

YIELD: 20 SERVINGS

1/2 cup sugar
1 cup white wine vinegar
1 cup water
1 tablespoon salt
1/4 teaspoon freshly ground pepper

3 large sweet onions, finely chopped
Mayonnaise
Softened butter
1 loaf very thinly sliced firm white
   bread, crusts trimmed

DISSOLVE the sugar in the wine vinegar and water in a covered container. STIR in the salt and pepper. ADD the onions and mix well. MARINATE, covered, in the refrigerator for 1 to 24 hours. DRAIN the onions, discarding the marinade. ADD enough mayonnaise to the onion mixture to make of a spreadable consistency. SPREAD the butter over the bread slices. SPREAD the onion mixture over 1/2 of the buttered slices. TOP with the remaining bread slices buttered side down. CUT into rectangles or triangles.

Pesto Ribbon Tea Sandwiches

YIELD: 12 SERVINGS

8 ounces cream cheese, softened
1/4 cup Basil Pesto
1/4 cup Sun-Dried Tomato Pesto

12 thin slices firm white bread, crusts trimmed

COMBINE 1/2 of the cream cheese and Basil Pesto in a small bowl and mix well. MIX the remaining cream cheese and Sun-Dried Tomato Pesto in a small bowl. SPREAD 4 slices of the bread with the Basil Pesto mixture. SPREAD 4 slices of the bread with the Sun-Dried Tomato Pesto mixture. STACK the Sun-Dried Tomato bread slices plain side down on top of the Basil Pesto bread slices. PLACE the remaining bread slices on top of each stack, forming four 3-layered sandwiches. CUT each into 3 rectangles.

BASIL PESTO

2 cups packed fresh basil leaves
1/4 cup pine nuts
3 or 4 garlic cloves, chopped

1/2 cup freshly grated Parmesan cheese
1/2 cup olive oil
Salt and freshly ground pepper to taste

PROCESS the basil, pine nuts, garlic and Parmesan cheese in a food processor until a thick paste forms. ADD the olive oil in a fine stream, processing constantly. SEASON with salt and pepper.

SUN-DRIED TOMATO PESTO

1 (8-ounce) jar oil-packed sun-dried tomatoes
1 large garlic clove, chopped
3 (1/4-x3-inch) strips orange zest

1/4 cup grated Parmesan cheese
1 1/2 teaspoons chopped fresh thyme leaves

DRAIN the sun-dried tomatoes, reserving the liquid. PROCESS the sun-dried tomatoes, garlic and orange zest in a food processor until finely chopped. ADD the Parmesan cheese and thyme. ADD the reserved liquid in a fine stream, processing constantly until the mixture is coarsely chopped.

Minced Ham and Pineapple Tea Sandwiches with Honey Butter

YIELD: 40 SERVINGS

Chicken and Smoked Almond Tea Sandwiches

YIELD: 12 SERVINGS

1 cup minced ham
1/2 cup chopped fresh or canned
   pineapple, drained
1 teaspoon Dijon mustard
Freshly ground pepper to taste

1 cup butter, softened
2 tablespoons honey
20 thin slices whole wheat bread,
   crusts trimmed

COMBINE the ham, pineapple, Dijon mustard and pepper in a mixer bowl and mix well. BEAT the butter and honey in a mixer bowl until smooth. SPREAD the honey butter on all the bread slices. SPREAD the ham mixture on 1/2 of the buttered bread slices. PLACE the remaining bread slices buttered side down on top of the ham mixture. CUT each sandwich into 4 triangles.

2 boneless skinless chicken breast
   halves, cooked, shredded
1/2 cup mayonnaise
2 tablespoons chopped shallot

1 teaspoon fresh rosemary
1/4 cup chopped smoked almonds
12 thin slices firm white bread, crusts
   trimmed

PROCESS the chicken, mayonnaise, shallot, rosemary and almonds in a food processor until of a spreadable consistency. SPREAD on 1/2 of the bread slices. TOP with the remaining bread slices. CUT into 2 rectangles or triangles.

Chive Puffs with Curried Chicken Filling

YIELD: 2½ DOZEN

1 cup water
½ cup butter
½ teaspoon salt
1 cup flour

4 eggs
½ teaspoon red pepper
1 tablespoon chopped fresh chives
Curried Chicken Filling

BRING the water, butter and salt to a boil in a medium saucepan. ADD the flour, stirring with a wooden spoon until the batter comes together in the center of the pan. REMOVE from the heat. ADD the eggs 1 at a time, beating well after each addition. ADD the red pepper and chives. SPOON into a pastry bag fitted with a number 5 tip. PIPE into 1-inch circles on baking sheets. BAKE at 350 degrees for 20 minutes or until golden brown. REMOVE from the oven and cut a slit in each puff. TURN off the oven. RETURN the puffs to the oven for 5 minutes. REMOVE from the oven to wire racks to cool. CUT the puffs into halves and remove doughy centers. FILL each with ½ tablespoon of Curried Chicken Filling.

CURRIED CHICKEN FILLING

2 boneless skinless chicken breast
   halves, roasted, shredded
½ to 1 tablespoon curry powder
⅛ teaspoon salt

¼ to ⅓ cup mayonnaise
¼ cup toasted chopped pecans or
   walnuts

PROCESS the chicken, curry powder and salt in a food processor. ADD enough mayonnaise gradually, processing until smooth and of the desired consistency. FOLD in the pecans.

Shrimp and Cucumber Tea Sandwiches

YIELD: 24 SERVINGS

$^1/_2$ hothouse cucumber
12 slices pumpernickel bread, cut into
    2-inch rounds
2 to 3 tablespoons butter, softened
$^1/_4$ cup mayonnaise

$^1/_2$ tablespoon finely chopped fresh
    tarragon or dill
24 medium shrimp, cooked, peeled
24 small tarragon leaves or sprigs
    of dill

PEEL the cucumber and cut into 24 thin slices. SPREAD each bread round with butter. TOP with a cucumber slice. MIX the mayonnaise and tarragon in a bowl. PIPE a small amount onto each cucumber. ARRANGE 1 shrimp on top of each. GARNISH each with a tarragon leaf.

NOTE: Each slice of bread should yield two 2-inch rounds.

Asparagus Frittata Squares

YIELD: 3 DOZEN

$1^1/_2$ pounds asparagus, cut into
    1-inch pieces
2 medium yellow onions, chopped
2 garlic cloves, minced
$^1/_2$ cup olive oil
1 cup dry bread crumbs

$1^1/_2$ cups grated Parmesan cheese
$^1/_2$ cup chopped fresh parsley
$1^1/_2$ teaspoons Italian seasoning
2 teaspoons salt
2 teaspoons freshly ground pepper
8 eggs, beaten

STEAM the asparagus in a steamer for 2 to 3 minutes or until tender-crisp. SAUTÉ the onions and garlic in the olive oil in a large skillet until tender. ADD the asparagus, bread crumbs, Parmesan cheese, parsley, Italian seasoning, salt and pepper and mix well. ADD the eggs and stir to mix well. POUR into a greased 9x13-inch baking dish. BAKE at 350 degrees for 40 to 45 minutes or until set and golden brown. CUT into bite-size squares to serve.

Watercress and Crabmeat Quiche

YIELD: 12 SERVINGS

1 recipe (1-crust) pie pastry
1 tablespoon whole grain mustard
1 bunch watercress, finely chopped
8 ounces cooked crabmeat
2 eggs
2 egg yolks
$3/4$ cup milk
$3/4$ cup heavy cream
2 tablespoons sherry
$1/4$ teaspoon freshly grated nutmeg
$1/8$ teaspoon cayenne
Salt to taste

BUTTER and flour an 8x12-inch tart pan with a removable bottom. ROLL the pastry $1/8$ inch thick on a generously floured surface. LINE the prepared pan with the pastry and prick the bottom with a fork. COVER the pastry with parchment paper or foil, leaving an overhang. FILL with pie weights. BAKE at 375 degrees for 20 minutes or until the edge is just beginning to brown. REMOVE the parchment paper and weights. BRUSH the pastry with the mustard. REDUCE the oven temperature to 325 degrees. MIX the watercress and crabmeat in a bowl. BEAT the eggs, egg yolks, milk and cream lightly in a mixer bowl. ADD the sherry, nutmeg, cayenne and salt. SPOON the crabmeat mixture into the prepared pastry shell. ADD the egg mixture, filling to within $1/4$ inch of the top. BAKE for 25 to 30 minutes or until the filling puffs. LET stand for 10 minutes before serving. REMOVE the quiche from the pan. SERVE warm or at room temperature.

Sweet Potato Biscuits with Spicy Turkey Pâté

YIELD: 16 SERVINGS

1/3 cup finely chopped green onions
1 garlic clove, minced
1/2 tablespoon olive oil
1 cup chopped cooked turkey
1 (8-ounce) can water chestnuts,
    drained, quartered
2 tablespoons mayonnaise
3 (1/2-inch) pieces crystallized ginger,
    coarsely chopped

1/4 teaspoon Creole seasoning
1 tablespoon rice wine vinegar
1 teaspoon soy sauce
Salt and freshly ground pepper
    to taste
Sweet Potato Biscuits
2 to 3 inner romaine lettuce leaves,
    torn into 1 1/2-inch pieces

SAUTÉ the green onions and garlic in the olive oil in a small skillet over medium heat for 2 to 3 minutes or until tender-crisp. COMBINE with the turkey, water chestnuts, mayonnaise, ginger, Creole seasoning, rice wine vinegar, soy sauce, salt and pepper in a food processor container. PROCESS until smooth. SPOON into a covered container. CHILL, covered, in the refrigerator. CUT the Sweet Potato Biscuits into halves. SPREAD the bottom halves with the turkey pâté. ADD a piece of lettuce. TOP with the remaining biscuit halves.

SWEET POTATO BISCUITS

1 cup all-purpose flour
1 cup cake flour
1 teaspoon salt
1 tablespoon brown sugar
1 tablespoon plus 1 teaspoon baking
    powder

1/4 cup unsalted butter, chopped
1 (15-ounce) can sweet potatoes,
    drained, mashed
1/3 to 1/2 cup half-and-half or milk
Melted butter
Paprika to taste

SIFT the flours, salt, brown sugar and baking powder together in a bowl. CUT in the butter until crumbly. ADD the sweet potatoes and just enough of the half-and-half to make a soft dough. KNEAD on a floured surface 3 or 4 times. PAT into a rectangle 1/2 inch thick. CUT into sixteen 1 1/2-inch squares. PLACE on a lightly greased baking sheet. BRUSH with melted butter. SPRINKLE with paprika. BAKE at 425 degrees for 10 to 15 minutes or until brown.

Coconut Scones

YIELD: 1 DOZEN

1³/₄ cups flour
2 teaspoons baking powder
1 tablespoon sugar
1 teaspoon salt
¹/₂ teaspoon baking soda

¹/₄ cup unsalted butter, chopped
¹/₂ cup sweetened flaked coconut
¹/₃ cup toasted pecan pieces
³/₄ to 1 cup coconut milk

SIFT the flour, baking powder, sugar, salt and baking soda into a large bowl. CUT in the butter until crumbly. STIR in the coconut and pecans. STIR in enough of the coconut milk to form a soft dough. PAT the dough on a floured surface into a circle ¹/₂ inch thick. CUT into 2-inch circles or squares. PLACE on an ungreased baking sheet. BAKE at 450 degrees for 10 to 15 minutes or until light brown. Serve with American Devonshire Cream (see page 19).

Sweet Lemon Cream Scones

YIELD: 2 DOZEN

2 cups flour
1 teaspoon salt
¹/₄ cup sugar
1 tablespoon baking powder
3 tablespoons butter
2 egg yolks, beaten

1 tablespoon finely chopped lemon
  balm
¹/₂ teaspoon freshly grated lemon peel
¹/₃ cup heavy cream
1 egg white, lightly beaten

MIX the flour, salt, sugar and baking powder in a bowl. CUT in the butter until crumbly. ADD the egg yolks, lemon balm and lemon peel to the cream and mix well. STIR into the flour mixture to form a soft dough. KNEAD on a floured surface about 20 times. ROLL the dough ¹/₂ inch thick. CUT into 2-inch circles. PLACE on ungreased baking sheets. BRUSH the tops with the egg white. BAKE at 450 degrees for 10 minutes or until light brown. STORE in an airtight container. SERVE with preserves and American Devonshire Cream (see page 19).

Lavender Sugar Scones

YIELD: 1 DOZEN

4 cups flour
1/4 cup Lavender Sugar
4 teaspoons baking powder
3/4 teaspoon salt
3/4 cup butter

1 egg yolk
1 cup milk
1/2 cup heavy cream
1 egg white, lightly beaten
1 tablespoon Lavender Sugar

MIX the flour, 1/4 cup Lavender Sugar, baking powder and salt in a bowl. CUT in the butter until crumbly. BEAT the egg yolk in a small bowl. STIR in the milk and cream. ADD to the flour mixture and mix to form a soft dough. TURN onto a lightly floured surface. KNEAD several times. ROLL into a circle 3/4 inch thick. CUT into 3-inch circles. PLACE 1 inch apart on a greased large baking sheet. PIERCE the tops with a fork. BRUSH with the egg white. SPRINKLE with 1 tablespoon Lavender Sugar. BAKE at 425 degrees for 15 to 18 minutes or until golden brown around the edges. REMOVE to a wire rack to cool.

Lavender Sugar

1 cup sugar

2 tablespoons dried lavender flowers

COMBINE the sugar and lavender flowers in a food processor container fitted with a chopping blade. PROCESS until the flowers are finely chopped. STORE in an airtight container.

American Devonshire Cream

YIELD: 1 1/2 CUPS

1/2 cup whipping cream
2 tablespoons confectioners' sugar

1/2 cup sour cream

BEAT the whipping cream in a chilled bowl until peaks are beginning to form. ADD the confectioners' sugar gradually, beating constantly. FOLD in the sour cream.

Miniature Chocolate Cheesecakes

YIELD: 2 DOZEN

1 cup chocolate cookie crumbs
2 tablespoons melted butter
6 ounces cream cheese, softened
$^1/_4$ cup sugar
1 egg

1 ounce semisweet chocolate, melted, cooled
1 teaspoon strong brewed coffee or liqueur (optional)
Confectioners' sugar

MIX the cookie crumbs and butter in a small bowl. SPOON 1 teaspoon of the crumb mixture into each of 24 paper-lined miniature muffin cups. PRESS the crumbs to the bottom of each cup using a paper liner. PROCESS the cream cheese, sugar, egg, chocolate and coffee in a food processor until smooth. SPOON into the prepared muffin cups, filling almost to the top. BAKE at 350 degrees for 20 minutes or until the tops begin to set and crack. REMOVE to a wire rack to cool. CHILL in the refrigerator. SPRINKLE with confectioners' sugar before serving.

Welsh Cheesecakes

YIELD: 2 DOZEN

1 recipe (2-crust) pie pastry
$^1/_2$ cup raspberry or apricot jam
$^3/_4$ cup flour
$^1/_2$ teaspoon baking powder
$^1/_4$ teaspoon salt
6 tablespoons butter or margarine, softened

$^1/_2$ cup sugar
1 egg
$^1/_2$ cup plus 1 tablespoon ground almonds
$^1/_4$ teaspoon vanilla extract
$^1/_4$ teaspoon almond extract
$^1/_4$ teaspoon lemon juice

LINE muffin cups with the pie pastry. PLACE 1 teaspoon of the jam in each pastry-lined cup. SIFT the flour, baking powder and salt together. CREAM the butter and sugar in a mixer bowl until light and fluffy. BEAT in the egg. ADD the ground almonds, vanilla, almond essence and lemon juice and mix well. FOLD in the flour mixture. SPOON over the jam in each muffin cup. BAKE at 375 degrees for 20 minutes or until set.

Miniature Lavender Cheesecakes

YIELD: 2 DOZEN

1 cup graham cracker crumbs
1 tablespoon sugar
2 tablespoons melted butter
2 tablespoons milk
2 teaspoons dried lavender flowers

8 ounces cream cheese, softened
1 egg
1/4 cup plus 2 tablespoons sugar
1/8 teaspoon almond extract

MIX the graham cracker crumbs, 1 tablespoon sugar and butter in a small bowl. SPOON 1 teaspoon of the crumb mixture into each of 24 paper-lined miniature muffin cups. PRESS the crumbs to the bottom of each cup using a paper liner. HEAT the milk in a small saucepan just to the boiling point. REMOVE from the heat. ADD the lavender flowers. LET steep for 1 hour. PRESS through a sieve, reserving the lavender milk and discarding the lavender flowers. PROCESS the cream cheese, egg, reserved lavender milk, 1/4 cup plus 2 tablespoons sugar and almond extract in a food processor until smooth. SPOON into the prepared muffin cups, filling almost to the top. BAKE at 375 degrees for 15 minutes or until set. LET stand until cool. CHILL, covered, in the refrigerator.

Fresh Fruit Fool in Chocolate Cups

YIELD: 4 DOZEN

2 cups chocolate chips, melted
2 cups fresh berries

1/2 cup sugar
1 1/2 cups whipping cream, whipped

BRUSH the chocolate on the insides of miniature foil baking cups with a small pastry brush until well coated. REPEAT 2 to 3 times to obtain a sturdy cup. LET stand until firm. LOOSEN the chocolate cups from the foil. RINSE the berries and drain well. COOK the fruit in a small saucepan over low heat for 30 minutes or until soft and juicy. MASH with a spoon. ADD the sugar. COOK until the sugar is dissolved, stirring constantly. PROCESS in a blender until puréed. FOLD in the whipped cream just before serving, leaving a marbled effect throughout. SPOON into the chocolate cups.

White Chocolate Mousse and Berry Trifle

YIELD: 12 TO 15 SERVINGS

1 envelope unflavored gelatin
$^1/_4$ cup cold water
7 ounces white chocolate squares
$^1/_2$ cup sugar
2 eggs
1 egg yolk
1 tablespoon sherry
2 cups whipping cream, whipped
1 angel food cake, cut into cubes
1 pint fresh strawberries, sliced
1 pint fresh raspberries
1 pint fresh blackberries
Fresh sprigs of mint

SPRINKLE gelatin over cold water in a 1-cup glass measure. LET stand for 2 minutes or until softened. MICROWAVE on High for 40 seconds. STIR for 2 minutes or until the gelatin is completely dissolved. COOL slightly. PLACE the white chocolate in a medium glass bowl. MICROWAVE on High for 1 to 2 minutes or until melted. STIR until smooth. COMBINE the sugar, eggs, egg yolk and sherry in a medium stainless steel bowl. PLACE the bowl over simmering water in a medium saucepan. BEAT for 5 minutes or until doubled in volume. BEAT in the dissolved gelatin. REMOVE from the heat. FOLD in the melted white chocolate. COOL to room temperature. FOLD in the whipped cream. RESERVE a few of the strawberries, raspberries and blackberries for garnish. LAYER $^1/_2$ of the cake cubes, $^1/_2$ of the remaining strawberries, $^1/_3$ of the white chocolate mousse, remaining raspberries and remaining blackberries in a trifle bowl. CONTINUE layers with $^1/_2$ of the remaining white chocolate mousse, remaining cake cubes, remaining strawberries and remaining white chocolate mousse. GARNISH with sprigs of fresh mint and the reserved berries.

Rosemary Apple Tea Cakes

YIELD: 3 DOZEN

1½ cups half-and-half

1 cup currants

½ cup plus 1 tablespoon unsalted butter

4 medium Granny Smith apples, peeled, diced

1 cup plus 2 tablespoons sugar

1 tablespoon chopped fresh rosemary

3 cups flour

4 teaspoons baking powder

1 teaspoon salt

2 eggs

Rosemary Whipped Cream

SCALD the half-and-half in a saucepan. REMOVE from the heat. STIR in the currants and ½ cup of the butter. LET stand until cool. SAUTÉ the apples in remaining 1 tablespoon butter and 2 tablespoons of the sugar in a saucepan for 3 to 4 minutes or until the apples are softened and glazed. ADD the rosemary. MIX the flour, remaining 1 cup sugar, baking powder and salt in a bowl. WHISK the eggs into the cooled half-and-half mixture. STIR into the flour mixture. ADD the apple mixture and mix just until moistened. SPOON into a buttered and floured 9x13-inch cake pan. BAKE at 350 degrees for 20 to 30 minutes or until a wooden pick inserted in the center comes out clean. INVERT onto a wire rack to cool. CUT the cake horizontally into halves. SPREAD the bottom half with Rosemary Whipped Cream. REPLACE the top half. CUT into small squares.

ROSEMARY WHIPPED CREAM

2 cups whipping cream

1 tablespoon finely ground rosemary

BEAT the whipping cream in a chilled mixer bowl until stiff. FOLD in the rosemary. SERVE immediately.

NOTE: Can substitute finely ground lavender or melted jelly for the rosemary.

Ginger Pound Cake

YIELD: 20 SERVINGS

3 cups flour
1 tablespoon ground ginger
$1/2$ teaspoon baking powder
$1/4$ teaspoon salt
$1^1/2$ cups butter or margarine,
  softened
$2^1/4$ cups packed brown sugar
$1/2$ cup sugar

5 eggs
2 teaspoons vanilla extract
1 cup milk
1 cup chopped toasted pecans
$1/2$ cup finely chopped crystallized
  ginger
Apple Marshmallow Glaze
Chopped toasted pecans

SIFT the flour, ground ginger, baking powder and salt together. CREAM the butter, brown sugar and sugar in a large mixer bowl until light and fluffy. ADD the eggs 1 at a time, beating well after each addition. BEAT in the vanilla. ADD the milk and flour mixture alternately, beating constantly after each addition. FOLD in 1 cup pecans and finely chopped ginger. SPOON into a greased and floured 10-inch tube pan. BAKE at 350 degrees for 1 hour and 10 minutes or until a wooden pick inserted in the center comes out clean. COOL in the pan for 15 minutes. INVERT onto a wire rack to cool completely. DRIZZLE Apple Marshmallow Glaze over the cooled cake. SPRINKLE chopped toasted pecans along the outside edge.

APPLE MARSHMALLOW GLAZE

16 large marshmallows
$2/3$ cup apple jelly
$1/4$ cup lemon juice

$1/4$ cup butter or margarine, cut into
  pieces

COMBINE the marshmallows, jelly and lemon juice in a medium saucepan. COOK over medium heat until smooth, stirring constantly. ADD the butter 1 piece at a time, whisking constantly until smooth.

Miniature Amaretto Fruitcakes

YIELD: 24 SERVINGS

Zest from 2 medium rough-skinned oranges
$^1/_4$ cup sugar
2 tablespoons water
$^1/_4$ cup amaretto
$^1/_2$ cup currants
$^1/_2$ cup finely chopped moist dried figs
$^1/_2$ cup unsalted butter, softened
$^2/_3$ cup sugar
$^1/_8$ teaspoon salt
1 egg
1 teaspoon vanilla extract
$^3/_4$ cup flour
$^1/_2$ cup chopped toasted pecans
Melted apricot jam

CHOP the orange zest finely. COMBINE with enough cold water to cover in a small saucepan. BRING to a boil and reduce the heat. SIMMER for 5 minutes and drain. ADD enough cold water to cover again. BRING to a boil and reduce the heat. SIMMER for 12 minutes and drain. ADD $^1/_4$ cup sugar and 2 table-spoons water. SIMMER for 10 to 12 minutes or until all the liquid has been absorbed. SPREAD in a thin layer on waxed paper. LET stand until dry. BRING the amaretto to a simmer in a small saucepan and remove from the heat. ADD the currants, figs and dry orange zest and mix well. CREAM the butter, $^2/_3$ cup sugar and salt in a mixer bowl for 2 to 3 minutes or until light and fluffy. ADD the egg and vanilla. BEAT for 2 minutes. FOLD in the flour $^1/_2$ at a time. FOLD in the pecans and fruit mixture. SPOON into lightly greased and floured minia-ture muffin pans. BAKE at 325 degrees for 25 to 30 minutes or until the fruitcakes test done. COOL in the pans for 5 minutes. REMOVE from the pans and brush the tops with melted apricot jam.

Lemon Macaroon Tarts

YIELD: 12 SERVINGS

1 egg
3/4 cup sugar
1 tablespoon plus 2 teaspoons
   cornstarch
Grated peel of 1 lemon
1/3 cup water

1/3 cup fresh lemon juice
2 to 3 drops of yellow food coloring
Macaroon Tart Shells
1/2 cup toasted flaked coconut
Mint leaves

BEAT the egg in a small bowl. COMBINE the sugar, cornstarch and lemon peel in a medium saucepan. WHISK in a mixture of the water and lemon juice. BRING to a boil over medium-high heat. BOIL for 1 minute, stirring constantly. STIR 1 to 2 spoonfuls of the hot mixture into the beaten egg. ADD the egg to the hot mixture. COOK for 1 to 2 minutes or until thickened, stirring constantly. ADD the food coloring 1 drop at a time until of the desired tint, stirring constantly. POUR into the Macaroon Tart Shells. GARNISH with toasted coconut and mint leaves.

MACAROON TART SHELLS

2 cups sweetened flaked coconut
2 egg whites
1/2 cup sugar

1/4 cup plus 2 tablespoons flour
1 teaspoon vanilla extract

SPRAY 12 muffin cups with nonstick cooking spray. COMBINE the coconut, egg whites, sugar, flour and vanilla in a bowl and mix well. PRESS into the prepared muffin cups, forming a shell. BAKE at 400 degrees for 15 to 18 minutes or until the edges are just beginning to turn brown. COOL in the pans for 2 to 3 minutes. LOOSEN the shells around the edges with a sharp knife. REMOVE carefully to wire racks to cool completely.

Butter Tarts

YIELD: 20 TO 24 SERVINGS

1 recipe (2-crust) pie pastry
3 eggs
2 cups packed brown sugar
2 tablespoons melted butter

1 tablespoon vanilla extract
1/2 cup currants or toasted chopped
    pecans

ROLL the pie pastry into a circle on a lightly floured surface. CUT into circles. FIT into miniature muffin cups. BEAT the eggs, brown sugar, butter and vanilla in a bowl until frothy. FOLD in the currants. POUR into the pastry-lined muffin cups. BAKE at 375 degrees for 25 to 35 minutes or until firm and lightly brown. SERVE hot or cold.

Molded Cream Cheese Mints

YIELD: ABOUT 1 1/4 POUNDS

1/4 cup margarine, softened
1/4 cup cream cheese, softened
1 tablespoon light corn syrup
1 tablespoon boiling water
1 (1-pound) package confectioners'
    sugar

Mint extract to taste
Food coloring
Sugar

BEAT the margarine and cream cheese in a mixer bowl until smooth. ADD the corn syrup and boiling water and beat well. ADD the confectioners' sugar. BEAT until a soft dough forms. ADD mint flavoring to taste. TINT as desired with food coloring. DIVIDE the dough into small balls. ROLL each ball in sugar to coat. PRESS into a candy mold. LET stand, covered, for 8 to 10 hours or until firm. UNMOLD the candy. MAY store in an airtight container in the refrigerator for up to 4 weeks.

Celebrated Beginnings

A WORK OF ART

MENU

PARMESAN PESTO DIP WITH FRESH CRUDITÉS – *PAGE 30*

BRIE WITH SUN-DRIED TOMATOES – *PAGE 35*

ISLANDER CHEESE SPREAD – *PAGE 35*

SPINACH AND MUSHROOM CHEESECAKE – *PAGE 36*

HAM BALLS IN SWEET-AND-SOUR CURRANT SAUCE – *PAGE 39*

ORANGE AND CINNAMON BISCOTTI – *PAGE 157*

WHITE CHOCOLATE BROWNIES – *PAGE 158*

CHOCOLATE MINT SQUARES – *PAGE 159*

OKINAWA WASSAIL – *PAGE 43*

Parmesan Pesto Dip

YIELD: ABOUT 3 CUPS

1½ cups sour cream
1 cup grated fresh Parmesan cheese
1 tablespoon olive oil
½ cup mayonnaise
2 tablespoons lemon juice
1 tablespoon finely chopped onion

½ cup coarsely chopped water chestnuts
¼ cup Basil Pesto (see page 12)
1 teaspoon Worcestershire sauce
Salt and pepper to taste

COMBINE the sour cream, Parmesan cheese, olive oil, mayonnaise, lemon juice and onion in a bowl and mix well. STIR in the water chestnuts, Basil Pesto, Worcestershire sauce, salt and pepper. CHILL, covered, in the refrigerator. SERVE with fresh crudités.

Skyline® Chili Dip

YIELD: 6 SERVINGS

8 ounces light cream cheese, softened
1 package Skyline® chili, thawed

1 bunch scallions, chopped
1 cup shredded sharp Cheddar cheese

SPREAD the cream cheese in a microwave-safe serving dish. MICROWAVE on High for 1½ minutes. POUR the chili over the cream cheese. MICROWAVE on High for 1½ minutes. SPRINKLE with the scallions and Cheddar cheese. MICROWAVE on High for 1½ minutes or until heated through. SERVE immediately with chips for dipping.

NOTE: Skyline® chili can be found in your grocery store's freezer case.

Spinach Artichoke Dip

YIELD: ABOUT 3 CUPS

2 cups mayonnaise
1 (10-ounce) package frozen spinach,
   thawed, drained
1 (14-ounce) can artichoke hearts,
   drained, chopped

1 (8-ounce) can water chestnuts,
   drained, chopped (optional)
1 teaspoon prepared horseradish
   (optional)
2 cups finely grated Parmesan cheese

COMBINE the mayonnaise, spinach, artichoke hearts and water chestnuts in a bowl and mix well. ADD the horseradish and Parmesan cheese and mix well. POUR into a glass baking dish. BAKE at 350 degrees for 20 to 35 minutes or until the top is brown. SERVE with bagel chips, thinly sliced French bread or crackers.

Black Bean Hummus

YIELD: ABOUT 2 CUPS

2 cups cooked black beans, or
   1 (15-ounce) can black beans,
   rinsed, drained
1/3 cup tahini
3 garlic cloves, minced
1/4 cup chopped red onion

1/3 cup olive oil
1/3 cup lemon juice
1/4 to 1/2 teaspoon cumin
Salt and freshly ground pepper
   to taste

PURÉE the black beans, tahini, garlic, red onion, olive oil, lemon juice, cumin, salt and pepper in a food processor. SPOON into a serving bowl. SERVE with toasted pita wedges.

Gazpacho Salsa with Creole Spiced Tortilla Chips

YIELD: 3 1/2 TO 4 CUPS

2 1/2 to 3 pounds tomatoes, chopped
1 hothouse or English cucumber, chopped
1 medium red onion, chopped
1 yellow bell pepper, chopped
1/2 bunch cilantro
2 jalapeños

2 garlic cloves
2 to 3 tablespoons olive oil
1 to 2 tablespoons red wine vinegar
1/2 to 1 teaspoon sugar
Salt and freshly ground pepper to taste
Creole Spiced Tortilla Chips

COMBINE the tomatoes, cucumber, red onion and yellow pepper in a bowl and toss to mix well. REMOVE the leaves from the cilantro and discard the stems. PROCESS the cilantro leaves, jalapeños, garlic, olive oil, red wine vinegar, sugar, salt and pepper in a blender until smooth. ADD to the vegetable mixture and mix well. CHILL, tightly covered, in the refrigerator. DRAIN slightly before serving. SERVE with Creole Spiced Tortilla Chips.

NOTE: Salsa may be stored for several days in the refrigerator.

CREOLE SPICED TORTILLA CHIPS

2 (10-count) packages 7-inch tortillas

1 to 2 tablespoons Creole seasoning or chili powder

CUT each package of tortillas into halves. CUT each half into 4 wedges. ARRANGE in single layers on baking sheets. SPRAY the wedges lightly with non-stick cooking spray. SPRINKLE with the Creole seasoning. BAKE at 350 degrees for 5 minutes. COOL and store in an airtight container.

Black-Eyed Pea Salsa

YIELD: 12 SERVINGS

4 (16-ounce) cans black-eyed peas, drained
8 green onions, chopped
1 red bell pepper, chopped
1 green bell pepper, chopped

1 jalapeño, chopped
1/2 bottle of zesty Italian salad dressing
Chopped cilantro to taste

COMBINE the black-eyed peas, green onions, red pepper, green pepper and jalapeño in a bowl and mix well. ADD the salad dressing and cilantro and mix well. CHILL, covered, in the refrigerator. SERVE with tortilla chips or as an accompaniment.

Summer Salsa

YIELD: 8 SERVINGS

4 ripe tomatoes, chopped
1 white onion, chopped
1/2 cup chopped cilantro
2 teaspoons salt

1/2 teaspoon black pepper
2 tablespoons olive oil
2 tablespoons red wine vinegar
1/8 teaspoon cayenne

COMBINE the tomatoes, onion, cilantro, salt, black pepper, olive oil, red wine vinegar and cayenne in a bowl and mix well. CHILL, covered, in the refrigerator for 8 to 12 hours. SERVE with tortilla chips.

NOTE: Can add one 15-ounce can black beans, rinsed and drained, one 10-ounce can corn, drained, and chopped red or green bell peppers.

Rumaki Pâté

YIELD: 1 CUP

Black Bean Pâté

YIELD: 15 TO 20 SERVINGS

Brie with Sun-Dried Tomatoes

YIELD: 16 SERVINGS

2 pounds Brie cheese, chilled
5 tablespoons minced parsley leaves
5 tablespoons freshly grated Parmesan
    cheese
2¹/₂ tablespoons sun-dried tomato oil

10 oil-packed sun-dried tomatoes,
    minced
12 garlic cloves, mashed
2 tablespoons minced fresh basil

REMOVE the rind from the top of the Brie cheese. PLACE the Brie cheese on a serving platter. COMBINE the parsley, Parmesan cheese, sun-dried tomato oil, sun-dried tomatoes, garlic and basil in a bowl and mix well. SPREAD on top of the Brie cheese. LET stand for 30 to 60 minutes at room temperature before serving. SERVE with plain water crackers or freshly sliced crusty French bread.

Islander Cheese Spread

YIELD: 16 TO 20 SERVINGS

¹/₂ fresh pineapple (sliced lengthwise)
16 ounces cream cheese, softened
2 tablespoons finely chopped green
    onions with tops

¹/₄ cup finely chopped green or red bell
    pepper
2 teaspoons seasoned salt
1 cup toasted chopped pecans

SCOOP the pineapple pulp into a food processor container, reserving the shell. DRAIN the reserved pineapple shell cut side down. PROCESS the pineapple pulp until crushed. BEAT the cream cheese in a mixer bowl until smooth. ADD the crushed pineapple and mix well. STIR in the green onions, green pepper, seasoned salt and ¹/₂ cup of the pecans. MOUND in the reserved pineapple shell. SPRINKLE with the remaining ¹/₂ cup pecans. SERVE with crackers.

NOTE: Can shape into a cheese ball and roll in the ¹/₂ cup pecans.

Spinach and Mushroom Cheesecake

YIELD: 25 SERVINGS

3/4 cup Italian bread crumbs
1/4 cup melted butter or margarine
1 (10-ounce) package chopped frozen spinach, thawed
1 cup chopped fresh mushrooms
1/4 cup finely chopped onion
2 garlic cloves, minced
1 (2-ounce) jar chopped pimento, drained
24 ounces cream cheese, softened
1 (7-ounce) package feta cheese, drained
1/3 cup milk
4 eggs
3/4 teaspoon salt
1/4 teaspoon ground red pepper
1/4 teaspoon black pepper
1/8 teaspoon ground nutmeg

BUTTER a 9-inch springform pan. SPRINKLE the sides with 1 tablespoon of the bread crumbs. MIX the remaining bread crumbs with 2 tablespoons of the butter in a bowl. PRESS into the prepared pan. DRAIN the spinach on paper towels. SAUTÉ the mushrooms, onion and garlic in the remaining 2 tablespoons butter in a large skillet over medium-high heat for 3 minutes or until tender. STIR in the spinach and pimento. REMOVE from the heat. BEAT the cream cheese at medium speed in a mixer bowl until smooth and creamy. ADD the feta cheese, beating until blended. ADD the milk gradually, beating constantly at low speed until blended. BEAT in the eggs 1 at a time. STIR in the spinach mixture, salt, red pepper, black pepper and nutmeg. POUR into the prepared pan. BAKE at 300 degrees for 1 hour or until almost set. TURN off the oven and leave the oven door partially open. LET stand for 1 hour. REMOVE the cheesecake to a wire rack and cool completely. CHILL, covered, in the refrigerator. REMOVE the side of the pan when ready to serve. SERVE with crackers.

Pesto Torte with Garlic Toasts

YIELD: ABOUT 25 SERVINGS

1 cup loosely packed, coarsely torn fresh spinach leaves
1 cup loosely packed, coarsely torn fresh basil leaves
1 teaspoon minced garlic
1/2 cup pitted kalamata or black olives
1/4 cup olive oil
1 cup freshly grated Parmesan cheese
12 ounces cream cheese, softened

1/4 cup chopped walnuts, toasted
1/2 cup chopped drained oil-pack sun-dried tomatoes
Freshly ground pepper to taste
1 sprig of basil
2 or 3 oil-pack whole sun-dried tomatoes
Garlic Toasts

LINE a 3-cup flat-bottom bowl or a 6-inch springform pan with plastic wrap, leaving a 4-inch overhang. PROCESS the spinach, basil, garlic and olives in a food processor until finely chopped. ADD the olive oil in a fine stream, processing constantly until smooth. ADD the Parmesan cheese and process until smooth. STIR the cream cheese in a small bowl until smooth. SPREAD 1/3 of the cream cheese in the bottom of the prepared bowl. LAYER the spinach mixture, walnuts, chopped sun-dried tomatoes and the remaining cream cheese 1/2 at a time over the cream cheese layer. FOLD the plastic wrap over the top. CHILL for 2 hours or up to 3 days; the flavor improves the longer the torte chills. UNWRAP the top. INVERT onto a serving plate. REMOVE the bowl and plastic wrap gently. SPRINKLE with pepper. GARNISH with a sprig of basil and whole sun-dried tomatoes. SERVE with Garlic Toasts.

GARLIC TOASTS

1/2 cup olive oil
1 garlic clove, finely chopped

2 baguettes, cut into 1/2-inch slices

HEAT the olive oil and garlic in a small saucepan for 2 to 3 minutes. BRUSH over the baguette slices. PLACE on baking sheets. BAKE at 350 degrees for 12 to 15 minutes or until golden brown. REMOVE to wire racks to cool.

NOTE: Can prepare several hours before serving.

Figgy Bleu Torte

YIELD: ABOUT 25 SERVINGS

12 ounces moist dried figs

¹/₂ teaspoon sugar

16 ounces cream cheese, softened

4 ounces bleu cheese, softened

LINE a 6-inch springform pan or flat-bottom bowl with plastic wrap, leaving an overhang. BOIL the figs in water to cover in a saucepan until soft; drain. COMBINE the figs and sugar in a food processor container. PROCESS until finely chopped. PROCESS the cream cheese and bleu cheese in a food processor until smooth. LAYER ¹/₂ of the cheese mixture, fig mixture and remaining cheese mixture in the prepared pan. FOLD the plastic wrap over the top. CHILL for 8 to 12 hours. UNWRAP the top. INVERT onto a serving plate. REMOVE the pan and plastic wrap gently. SERVE with plain crackers.

Salmon Ball

YIELD: ABOUT 25 SERVINGS

1 (16-ounce) can red salmon, drained

8 ounces cream cheese, softened

1 tablespoon lemon juice

2 teaspoons onion, grated

1 teaspoon prepared horseradish

¹/₄ teaspoon salt

¹/₄ teaspoon liquid smoke

¹/₂ cup chopped pecans

3 tablespoons minced parsley

FLAKE the salmon in a bowl. ADD the cream cheese, lemon juice, onion, horse-radish, salt and liquid smoke and mix well. CHILL, covered, for several hours. MIX the pecans and parsley together. SHAPE the salmon mixture into a ball. ROLL in the pecan mixture. CHILL, covered, until serving time.

Italian Crostini

YIELD: ABOUT 24 SERVINGS

1 French or sourdough baguette, cut into ¹/₂-inch slices
1 (16-ounce) can white beans, drained
1 tablespoon butter
Salt and pepper to taste

2 to 3 tablespoons Italian salad dressing
¹/₂ red bell pepper, finely chopped
2 to 3 scallions, finely chopped
1 cup finely shredded mozzarella cheese

PLACE the baguette slices on a baking sheet. BAKE at 350 degrees for 5 minutes. TURN over the slices. BAKE for 5 minutes longer or until toasted. SAUTÉ the beans in the butter in a small sauté pan until softened. ADD the salt and pepper and salad dressing and mix well. POUR into a bowl. MASH the beans until smooth. FOLD in the red pepper and scallions. PLACE 1 tablespoon of the bean mixture on each toasted baguette slice. SPRINKLE with cheese. PLACE on a baking sheet. BROIL for 1 to 1¹/₂ minutes or until the cheese begins to melt.

Ham Balls in Sweet-and-Sour Currant Sauce

YIELD: ABOUT 10 SERVINGS

12 ounces fresh ground pork
8 ounces ground cooked ham
1 cup cracker or bread crumbs
1 egg
³/₄ cup milk
¹/₂ teaspoon salt

¹/₂ cup packed brown sugar
¹/₄ cup cider vinegar
¹/₄ cup hot water
¹/₂ teaspoon dry mustard
2 tablespoons currants

MIX the pork, ham, cracker crumbs, egg, milk and salt in a bowl. SHAPE into 1¹/₂-inch balls. PLACE in a lightly greased 9x13-inch baking pan. COMBINE the brown sugar, cider vinegar, water, dry mustard and currants in a saucepan. COOK over low heat until the sugar and mustard dissolves, stirring constantly. POUR over the ham balls. BAKE at 325 degrees for 50 minutes or until cooked through, basting with the sauce every 10 minutes. SERVE immediately.

Ham Puffs

YIELD: 5 DOZEN

1 cup water
1/2 cup butter or margarine
1 cup flour
4 eggs
1 (4-ounce) can deviled ham

3 ounces cream cheese, softened
2 tablespoons finely chopped green
  bell pepper
1 1/2 teaspoons prepared horseradish
1 teaspoon lemon juice

BRING the water and butter to a boil in a saucepan. STIR in the flour immediately. REDUCE the heat to low. COOK for 1 minute or until the mixture leaves the side of the pan, stirring constantly. REMOVE from the heat. ADD the eggs 1 at a time, beating until smooth after each addition. DROP by rounded teaspoonfuls 1 1/2 inches apart on ungreased baking sheets. BAKE at 400 degrees for 25 minutes. REMOVE to wire racks to cool. CUT slits in the puffs and remove doughy centers. COMBINE the deviled ham, cream cheese, green pepper, horseradish and lemon juice in a bowl and mix well. SPOON into the puffs.

Shrimp Nachos

YIELD: 15 TO 20 SERVINGS

1 package round tortilla chips
1 package frozen salad shrimp,
  thawed
2 to 3 tablespoons chopped green
  onions

2 tablespoons chopped green chiles
1/4 cup mayonnaise
1 to 1 1/2 cups shredded Colby-
  Monterey Jack cheese

PLACE the tortilla chips in a large baking dish. COMBINE the shrimp, green onions, green chiles, mayonnaise and cheese in a bowl and mix well. SPOON over the tortilla chips. BAKE at 350 degrees until the cheese is melted and bubbly.

NOTE: Topping can be prepared ahead and refrigerated until needed.

Southern Cheese Straws

YIELD: 14 DOZEN

1 cup butter, softened
1 pound grated sharp Cheddar
  cheese, at room temperature
2½ cups flour

1 teaspoon baking powder
1 teaspoon salt
½ to 1 teaspoon cayenne

COMBINE the butter and cheese in a bowl and mix well. ADD the flour, baking powder, salt and cayenne and mix well. PLACE in a cookie press fitted with a star tip. PRESS into 2-inch straws onto ungreased baking sheets. BAKE at 350 degrees for 10 to 15 minutes or until firm. WATCH carefully to prevent over-baking. COOL on wire racks. STORE in an airtight container.

Doc's Bloody Marys

YIELD: 4 SERVINGS

1 (32-ounce) can clamato juice,
  chilled
10 ounces vodka
10 drops of Tabasco sauce
2 tablespoons Worcestershire sauce

½ teaspoon lime juice
¼ teaspoon salt
¼ teaspoon freshly ground pepper
Fresh lime wedges

COMBINE the clamato juice, vodka, Tabasco sauce, Worcestershire sauce, lime juice, salt and pepper in a large pitcher and mix well. POUR into chilled glasses. GARNISH with fresh lime wedges.

Peach Sangria

YIELD: 2 QUARTS

Chocolate Mocha Punch

YIELD: 20 SERVINGS

8 large strawberries
2 peaches, peeled, thinly sliced
1 (750-milliliter) bottle Vouvray or
   other fruity white wine

1 (12-ounce) can apricot nectar
   (about 1½ cups), chilled
1 (16-ounce) bottle sparkling peach
   flavored water, chilled

REMOVE the stems from the strawberries. CUT the strawberries into quarters. COMBINE the strawberries, peaches and wine in a 2-quart pitcher or container. CHILL, covered, for 2 hours. STIR in the apricot nectar and sparkling water just before serving.

NOTE: Can substitute one 8-ounce package frozen sliced peaches for the fresh.

7 cups cold brewed coffee
2 quarts chocolate ice cream
¼ cup rum (optional)

¼ teaspoon salt
2 cups whipping cream, whipped

COMBINE the coffee and 1 quart of the ice cream in a large mixer bowl and beat until smooth. ADD the rum and salt and mix well. POUR into a punch bowl. FOLD in the remaining 1 quart ice cream and whipped cream just before serving. LADLE into punch cups.

NOTE: When doubling the recipe, do not double the whipped cream.

Winter's Treat Hot Buttered Rum Mix

YIELD: 100 SERVINGS

½ gallon vanilla ice cream, softened
2 cups butter, softened

1 (1-pound) package brown sugar

COMBINE the ice cream, butter and brown sugar in a covered freezer container and mix well. STORE, tightly covered, in the freezer. TO serve, combine about 2 tablespoons of the ice cream mixture with 1 shot rum and 6 ounces boiling water in a large heavy mug.

Okinawa Wassail

YIELD: 30 TO 40 SERVINGS

6 tea bags
1 quart boiling water
2 (750-milliliter) bottles cabernet
sauvignon or burgundy

1 gallon apple juice
6 cinnamon sticks
12 whole cloves
12 whole allspice

STEEP the tea bags in the boiling water in an 8-quart stockpot for 5 minutes. REMOVE the tea bags. ADD the wine, apple juice, cinnamon sticks, cloves and allspice. SIMMER for 30 minutes or longer. STRAIN before serving.

Salads and Soups

LET'S DO LUNCH

MENU

CHICKEN SALAD NORTHWOODS – *PAGE 48*

WHITE GAZPACHO – *PAGE 58*

PINEAPPLE MUFFINS – *PAGE 133*

CARROT LAYER CAKE WITH CREAM CHEESE FROSTING – *PAGE 145*

THE FOUNTAIN AT SCHILLER PARK IN GERMAN VILLAGE

Originally a neoclassic statue of the goddess Hebe, the original Umbrella Girl statue mysteriously disappeared from Schiller Park decades ago. After a futile search, the German Village Society dedicated itself to replacing the statue. Nationally renowned Columbus sculptor Joan Wobst contributed her time and talents to creating the Victorian German fountain that graces Schiller Park today. It is easy for visitors to imagine the darling little fräulein, whose back is placed to Stewart Avenue School, enjoying a stroll through the park on her way home from school.

Marinated Steak Salad

YIELD: 8 SERVINGS

2 pounds boneless sirloin steak
Mustard Vinaigrette
4 ounces shallots, chopped
1 (14-ounce) can hearts of palm,
 drained, sliced 1/2 inch thick

8 ounces mushrooms, sliced
2 tablespoons freshly chopped chives
2 tablespoons freshly chopped parsley
1 teaspoon dried dill
2 heads romaine lettuce, torn

COMBINE the steak with half the Mustard Vinaigrette in a large sealable plastic bag. COMBINE the shallots, hearts of palm, mushrooms, chives, parsley and dill with the remaining Mustard Vinaigrette in a large sealable plastic bag. PLACE both bags in the refrigerator and marinate for 8 to 24 hours. DRAIN the steak and grill until done to taste. SLICE thinly on the diagonal and cool to room temperature. COMBINE the lettuce with the marinated vegetables in a large bowl and toss to coat well. SPOON the salad onto serving plates and top with the steak.

MUSTARD VINAIGRETTE

1 egg or equivalent egg substitute
3 tablespoons tarragon vinegar
1 1/2 teaspoons fresh lemon juice
1 tablespoon Dijon mustard
1/8 teaspoon Tabasco sauce

1 teaspoon Worcestershire sauce
1 teaspoon salt
1/4 teaspoon freshly ground pepper
1/3 cup olive oil

COMBINE the egg, tarragon vinegar, lemon juice, Dijon mustard, Tabasco sauce, Worcestershire sauce, salt and pepper in a blender or food processor container; process until smooth. ADD the olive oil in a fine stream, processing constantly until smooth.

Fiesta Chicken Salad

YIELD: 6 SERVINGS

4 boneless skinless chicken breast halves
1 medium jalapeño, seeded, minced
1 medium garlic clove, minced
1 teaspoon Dijon mustard
$1/2$ teaspoon chili powder
$1/4$ teaspoon salt
$1/8$ teaspoon freshly ground pepper
$1/2$ teaspoon hot pepper sauce
3 tablespoons red wine vinegar
$1/3$ cup olive oil
4 large Roma tomatoes, seeded, chopped
2 green onions, thinly sliced
1 cup sliced black olives
$3/4$ cup shredded Monterey Jack cheese or Cheddar cheese
8 large romaine lettuce leaves, shredded

COMBINE the chicken with water to cover in a saucepan; bring to a boil. COVER and reduce the heat. SIMMER for 10 to 15 minutes or until cooked through. DRAIN and cool. CHOP the chicken and place in a large bowl. COMBINE the jalapeño, garlic, Dijon mustard, chili powder, salt, pepper, hot pepper sauce and red wine vinegar in a food processor container. ADD the olive oil in a fine stream, processing constantly until blended. SPOON 2 tablespoons of the dressing over the chicken and toss to coat well. ADD the tomatoes, green onions, olives, shredded cheese, romaine lettuce and remaining dressing and toss well. SERVE immediately.

Chicken Salad Northwoods

YIELD: 6 SERVINGS

5$\frac{1}{2}$ cups chicken stock
3 chicken bouillon cubes
1 cup uncooked wild rice
Juice of $\frac{1}{2}$ lemon
1 chicken breast, cooked, chopped
3 green onions, sliced

$\frac{1}{2}$ red bell pepper, chopped
2 ounces uncooked sugar peas,
    cut into 1-inch pieces
Dijon Vinaigrette
2 avocados, coarsely chopped
1 cup pecans halves, toasted

COMBINE the chicken stock and bouillon cubes in a saucepan and bring to a boil. ADD the wild rice and reduce the heat. SIMMER for 45 minutes; drain and cool to room temperature. TOSS the rice with lemon juice in a bowl. ADD the chicken, green onions, bell pepper and peas. ADD the Dijon Vinaigrette and toss to coat well. CHILL, covered, for 2 to 4 hours. ADD the avocados and pecans at serving time and toss gently.

DIJON VINAIGRETTE

2 garlic cloves, minced
1 tablespoon Dijon mustard
$\frac{1}{4}$ cup rice vinegar
$\frac{1}{4}$ teaspoon sugar

$\frac{1}{2}$ teaspoon salt
$\frac{1}{2}$ teaspoon pepper
$\frac{1}{3}$ cup vegetable oil

COMBINE the garlic, Dijon mustard, rice vinegar, sugar, salt and pepper in a blender container and process until smooth. ADD the vegetable oil in a fine stream, processing constantly until smooth.

Crabmeat-Stuffed Avocados

YIELD: 4 SERVINGS

2 medium avocados
1 cup Cheddar Cheese Sauce
1 (9-ounce) package frozen artichoke
    hearts, cooked, cut into halves

1½ cups chopped crabmeat, or
    a combination of shrimp
    and crabmeat
1 cup shredded Cheddar cheese

CUT the avocados into halves. SCOOP the avocado out of the shells, reserving the shells; chop the avocado. COMBINE the Cheddar Cheese Sauce, artichokes and crabmeat in a bowl and mix well. FOLD in the chopped avocado. SPOON into the reserved avocado shells and place on a baking sheet. SPRINKLE with the cheese. BAKE at 350 degrees for 10 to 12 minutes or until bubbly.

NOTE: Can substitute canned artichoke hearts for frozen.

CHEDDAR CHEESE SAUCE

2 tablespoons butter
2 tablespoons flour
Mrs. Dash seasoning to taste

Pepper to taste
1 cup milk
1 cup shredded Cheddar cheese

MELT the butter in a saucepan. STIR in the flour, Mrs. Dash seasoning and pepper. COOK over medium heat until bubbly, stirring constantly. STIR in the milk. COOK until thickened, stirring constantly. ADD the cheese and stir until melted.

Curried Tuna Salad

YIELD: 8 SERVINGS

2 (7-ounce) cans tuna
1/2 (8-ounce) jar pimento-stuffed olives
1 tablespoon chopped onion
1 (7-ounce) can sliced water
   chestnuts, drained
2 hard-cooked eggs, chopped

1/2 cup mayonnaise
1/2 cup sour cream
1/4 cup lemon juice
1 tablespoon curry powder
1 tablespoon salt
Sliced olives

COMBINE the tuna, olives, onion, water chestnuts and eggs in a bowl. ADD the mayonnaise, sour cream, lemon juice, curry powder and salt; mix gently. GARNISH with sliced olives.

Sesame Broccoli Salad

YIELD: 4 SERVINGS

Florets of 2 stalks broccoli
2 cups ice
1/4 cup sesame oil
2 tablespoons red pepper flakes
2 garlic cloves, minced

2 teaspoons red wine vinegar or
   balsamic vinegar
1/3 cup olive oil
1 tablespoon salt

BLANCH the broccoli in boiling water in a large saucepan for 2 minutes. REMOVE from the heat and add 2 cups ice to cool quickly; drain and place in a salad bowl. HEAT the sesame oil in a small saucepan over medium heat until warm. REMOVE from the heat and add the red pepper flakes; let stand for 10 minutes. POUR over the broccoli and toss to coat well. COMBINE the garlic, red wine vinegar, olive oil and salt in a bowl and mix well. ADD to the broccoli and toss gently. CHILL, covered, for 2 hours or longer.

Tarragon Potato Salad

YIELD: 10 SERVINGS

10 medium red potatoes
  (about 3 pounds)
$1/2$ beef bouillon cube
$1/4$ cup warm water
$1/2$ cup mayonnaise
$1/4$ cup cider vinegar

$1/4$ cup chopped green onions
2 tablespoons minced fresh parsley
2 teaspoons minced fresh tarragon, or
  $1/2$ teaspoon dried tarragon
Salt and pepper to taste

COOK the unpeeled potatoes in water to cover in a saucepan for 20 minutes or until tender; drain and cool slightly. CUT into $1/4$-inch slices. DISSOLVE the bouillon cube in the warm water. COMBINE with the mayonnaise, cider vinegar, green onions, parsley, tarragon, salt and pepper in a bowl and whisk until smooth. ADD the potatoes and toss gently. CHILL, covered, for several hours.

Tomato Bread Salad

YIELD: 4 SERVINGS

1 baguette
2 or 3 garlic cloves, minced
$1/4$ cup olive oil
10 to 12 Roma tomatoes, seeded, cut
  into $3/4$-inch pieces

1 medium sweet or red onion,
  chopped
$1/4$ cup chopped fresh basil
$1/4$ cup red wine vinegar
$1/2$ cup olive oil

CUT the baguette into halves lengthwise; cut the halves into halves lengthwise to make 4 long pieces. SAUTÉ the garlic lightly in the olive oil in a small saucepan. BRUSH the cut sides of the bread with the garlic oil and place on a baking sheet. BAKE at 300 degrees for 30 minutes or until golden brown. CUT into croutons. DRAIN the tomatoes in a colander. COMBINE with the onion and basil in a large bowl. WHISK the red wine vinegar and olive oil in a small bowl. POUR over the tomato mixture and mix gently. ADD the croutons at serving time.

Romaine Salad with Sweet and Tangy Mustard Dressing

YIELD: 6 SERVINGS

1/3 cup sugar
4 ounces slivered almonds
1 head romaine lettuce, torn
1 head red leaf lettuce, torn

White portions of 1 bunch green
   onions, thinly sliced
Sweet and Tangy Mustard Dressing

MELT the sugar in a small heavy skillet over high heat. COOK until golden brown, stirring constantly with a wooden spoon. ADD the almonds and stir to coat well. POUR onto foil and let stand until cool. COMBINE the romaine lettuce and red leaf lettuce in a large bowl. ADD the green onions and Sweet and Tangy Mustard Dressing and toss to coat well. BREAK up the caramelized almonds and sprinkle over the salad.

SWEET AND TANGY MUSTARD DRESSING

2 teaspoons Dijon mustard
3 tablespoons sugar
1/2 teaspoon salt

3 tablespoons malt vinegar
3/4 cup vegetable oil

COMBINE the Dijon mustard, sugar, salt, malt vinegar and vegetable oil in a blender or food processor container. PROCESS until smooth. USE immediately or chill in the blender container until serving time and process briefly to mix well before serving.

Green Salad with Jicama and Orange Poppy Seed Dressing

YIELD: 8 SERVINGS

4 ounces pine nuts
1 medium jicama
Assorted salad greens for 8 servings

1 medium red onion, thinly sliced
Sections of 4 large oranges
Orange Poppy Seed Dressing

TOAST the pine nuts lightly in a small skillet; let stand until cool. PEEL the jicama and cut into $1/4$-inch slices. CUT into desired shapes with canapé cutters. COMBINE the salad greens, jicama, onion, oranges and pine nuts in a salad bowl. ADD the Orange Poppy Seed Dressing and toss to coat well.

ORANGE POPPY SEED DRESSING

6 tablespoons sugar
Grated peel of 2 large rough-skinned
  oranges
$1/2$ cup fresh orange juice
$1/4$ cup white wine vinegar

2 tablespoons minced shallots
$1/2$ teaspoon freshly ground pepper
$2/3$ cup vegetable or canola oil
2 tablespoons poppy seeds (optional)

COMBINE the sugar, orange peel, orange juice, white wine vinegar, shallots and pepper in a blender or food processor container; process until smooth. ADD the vegetable oil in a fine stream, processing constantly until smooth. COMBINE with the poppy seeds in a container with a tightfitting lid. COVER and shake to mix. STORE in the refrigerator for up to 1 week.

Strawberry Spinach Salad with Poppy Seed Dressing

YIELD: 6 SERVINGS

1 pound fresh spinach, torn
1 pint fresh strawberries, sliced
Poppy Seed Dressing

$^1/_2$ cup chopped walnuts or pecans, toasted
$^1/_2$ cup crumbled bleu cheese

COMBINE the spinach and strawberries in a salad bowl. ADD the Poppy Seed Dressing just before serving and toss to coat well. TOP with the walnuts and bleu cheese.

POPPY SEED DRESSING

$^1/_2$ cup sugar
2 tablespoons sesame seeds
1 tablespoon poppy seeds
1$^1/_2$ teaspoons minced Vidalia onion

$^1/_4$ teaspoon Worcestershire sauce
$^1/_4$ cup cider vinegar
$^1/_4$ teaspoon paprika
$^1/_2$ cup vegetable oil

COMBINE the sugar, sesame seeds, poppy seeds, onion, Worcestershire sauce, cider vinegar and paprika in a small jar with a lid. COVER and shake until the sugar is completely dissolved. ADD the vegetable oil and shake until well mixed. CHILL for 1 hour or longer. SHAKE again at serving time.

Spanish Salad Dressing

YIELD: $^3/_4$ CUP

1 small white onion, coarsely chopped
$^2/_3$ cup sugar
$^1/_3$ cup white vinegar
1 cup salad oil

1 teaspoon salt
$^1/_2$ teaspoon ground pepper
1 teaspoon celery seed
1 teaspoon prepared mustard

Process all ingredients in a blender or food processor until well mixed. Refrigerate until ready to use over mixed salad greens.

Mediterranean Pasta Salad

YIELD: 6 SERVINGS

2 tablespoons vegetable oil
2 tablespoons olive oil
1 tablespoon fresh lemon juice
1 tablespoon red wine vinegar
1 garlic clove, minced
1 teaspoon sugar
$1/2$ teaspoon dried oregano

$1/8$ teaspoon freshly ground pepper
6 ounces uncooked penne
$1/3$ cup sliced green onions
$1/3$ cup kalamata olives
2 ounces feta cheese, crumbled
$1/4$ cup chopped oil-pack sun-dried
    tomatoes, drained

COMBINE the vegetable oil, olive oil, lemon juice, red wine vinegar, garlic, sugar, oregano and pepper in a blender container or covered jar and process or shake until well mixed. COOK the pasta using the package directions; drain. COMBINE with the green onions, olives, feta cheese and sun-dried tomatoes in a bowl. ADD the dressing and toss to mix well. CHILL until serving time.

Italian Pasta Salad

YIELD: 12 SERVINGS

1 pound uncooked rotini
2 cups broccoli florets
1 medium tomato, chopped
1 medium green bell pepper, chopped
$1/2$ medium red onion, finely chopped
1 small zucchini, chopped
1 (8-ounce) can black olives, chopped

$3/4$ cup grated Parmesan cheese
$1 1/3$ cups extra-virgin olive oil
$2/3$ cup red wine vinegar
4 garlic cloves, finely minced
2 teaspoons dry mustard
$1 1/2$ teaspoons salt
Pepper to taste

COOK the pasta using the package directions; rinse and drain. COMBINE with the broccoli, tomato, green pepper, red onion, zucchini, black olives and Parmesan cheese in a large bowl. COMBINE the olive oil, red wine vinegar, garlic, dry mustard, salt and pepper in a jar with a lid; cover and shake until slightly thickened. ADD all but $1/2$ cup of the dressing to the salad and toss lightly to mix well. CHILL until serving time. ADD the remaining $1/2$ cup dressing at serving time and toss again.

Christmas Fruit Salad Mold

YIELD: 10 TO 12 SERVINGS

1 (6-ounce) package raspberry gelatin
1 cup boiling water
1 (16-ounce) can whole cranberry
   sauce
1 (20-ounce) can Bing cherries

1 (20-ounce) can crushed pineapple
1 unpeeled large apple, chopped
3/4 cup chopped celery
1/2 cup chopped pecans

DISSOLVE the gelatin in the boiling water in a large bowl. ADD the cranberry sauce and undrained cherries and pineapple. STIR in the apple, celery and pecans. SPOON into a 9x13-inch dish and chill until set. CUT into squares. SERVE on lettuce leaves.

Cranberry Congealed Salad

YIELD: 8 SERVINGS

2 (3-ounce) packages wild raspberry
   gelatin
1 cup boiling water
2 cups sugar
1 cup cold water

1 (12-ounce) package cranberries,
   ground
2 unpeeled medium oranges, ground
1 cup crushed walnuts

DISSOLVE the gelatin in the boiling water in a bowl. ADD the sugar and stir until dissolved. STIR in the cold water. ADD the cranberries, oranges and walnuts and mix well. SPOON into a mold or dish. CHILL until set. UNMOLD or cut into squares to serve.

NOTE: Can substitute 1 package black raspberry gelatin for 1 package of the wild raspberry gelatin if preferred.

Spinach Mint Soup

YIELD: 4 TO 6 SERVINGS

1 onion, finely chopped
3 tablespoons butter or margarine
3 cups chicken broth
1 (10-ounce) package frozen
   small peas
1 (10-ounce) package frozen chopped
   spinach, thawed, well drained

1/2 cup fresh mint leaves
1 cup milk or cream
Salt and pepper to taste
Grated nutmeg (optional)

SAUTÉ the onion in the butter in a saucepan over medium heat for 20 minutes or until tender. ADD the chicken broth, peas and spinach. SIMMER for 20 minutes. ADD the mint. SIMMER for 5 minutes longer. STRAIN the soup, reserving the vegetables and liquid. PROCESS the reserved vegetables in a food processor until smooth. COMBINE with the reserved liquid and milk in the saucepan. COOK until heated through. SEASON with salt and pepper to taste. TOP with grated nutmeg.

NOTE: This soup can also be served cold.

Strawberry Soup

YIELD: 4 SERVINGS

1 quart strawberries, sliced, or
   1 (10-ounce) package frozen
   juice-pack strawberries
2 cups plain yogurt
1/4 cup confectioners' sugar

2 tablespoons dry white wine, and/or
   4 to 6 tablespoons lime juice
Grenadine syrup to taste
Sliced strawberries
Sprigs of mint

PROCESS 1 quart strawberries in a food processor until smooth. STRAIN to remove the seeds. COMBINE the strained purée with the yogurt, confectioners' sugar, white wine and grenadine syrup in the food processor container and process until smooth. CHILL for 1 to 2 hours. GARNISH servings with additional strawberry slices and a sprig of mint.

Kelton House
Gazpacho

YIELD: 4 SERVINGS

1 large sweet onion
2 green bell peppers
10 to 12 Roma tomatoes
1 English cucumber
5 or 6 garlic cloves, minced
½ cup olive oil
1 tablespoon Worcestershire sauce

1 to 2 teaspoons dried ground
    coriander, or to taste
1 tablespoon kosher salt, or to taste
2 cups tomato juice or vegetable juice
    cocktail
Hot pepper sauce to taste

CHOP the onion, green peppers, tomatoes and cucumber separately in a food processor, removing to a large bowl; do not purée. COMBINE the garlic, olive oil, Worcestershire sauce, coriander, kosher salt and 1 cup of the tomato juice in the food processor container and process until smooth. ADD to the vegetables and mix well. ADD enough of the remaining tomato juice to make of the desired consistency. SEASON with the hot pepper sauce. CHILL for 2 hours or longer to blend the flavors.

White Gazpacho

YIELD: 6 SERVINGS

3 cucumbers, peeled, coarsely
    chopped
1 garlic clove, crushed
3 cups chicken broth
3 tablespoons white vinegar

2 cups sour cream, reduced-fat sour
    cream or yogurt
1 teaspoon salt
Sliced almonds, chopped green onions,
    parsley or bacon

COMBINE the cucumbers, garlic and chicken broth in a food processor container and process until smooth. POUR into a large bowl. WHISK in the vinegar, sour cream and salt. CHILL, covered, for 8 hours to 3 days. GARNISH servings with almonds, green onions, parsley or bacon.

NOTE: Can add chopped tomatoes if desired.

Black Bean Soup

YIELD: 4 TO 6 SERVINGS

1 (12-ounce) package black beans
8 cups vegetable or chicken stock
8 ounces bacon, cooked, crumbled, or 1 ham bone
1 large onion, chopped
4 carrots, shredded
2 ribs celery, chopped
2 garlic cloves, minced
1 green bell pepper, chopped
Olive oil or bacon drippings
1 (15-ounce) can tomato sauce or puréed tomatoes
4 bay leaves
4 jalapeños, chopped (optional)
Salt and pepper to taste
Sour cream

SORT and rinse the beans; drain. COMBINE the beans, vegetable stock and bacon in a stockpot. BRING to a boil and reduce the heat. SIMMER, covered, for 2^1/$_2$ hours. SAUTÉ the onion, carrots, celery, garlic and green pepper in a small amount of olive oil in a skillet until the onion is transparent. ADD the sautéed vegetables, tomato sauce, bay leaves and jalapeños to the beans and mix well. SEASON with salt and pepper. COOK until tender. DISCARD the bay leaves. GARNISH servings with sour cream.

NOTE: Can process the soup in a food processor until puréed before serving. Can cook in a slow cooker on High for 6 hours.

Carrot Soup

YIELD: 6 SERVINGS

3 cups sliced carrots
2¹/₂ cups chicken or vegetable broth
2 tablespoons margarine
3 whole cloves
¹/₄ teaspoon coriander
¹/₂ teaspoon sugar

¹/₄ teaspoon salt
¹/₈ teaspoon white pepper
1 cup evaporated milk, whole milk or
     half-and-half
Chopped parsley or herbed croutons

COMBINE the carrots, chicken broth, margarine, cloves, coriander, sugar, salt and white pepper in a saucepan. COOK for 30 minutes. POUR into a food processor container and process until smooth. HEAT the evaporated milk just to the simmering point in a saucepan. ADD the puréed mixture. COOK until heated through. GARNISH servings with chopped parsley or herbed croutons.

Vermont Cheddar Soup

YIELD: 4 TO 6 SERVINGS

1 large carrot, sliced
¹/₂ cup chopped onion
2 ribs celery, sliced
2 tablespoons margarine
¹/₄ cup flour
3 cups chicken stock

¹/₂ cup heavy cream
2 cups shredded Cheddar cheese
¹/₂ teaspoon Worcestershire sauce
Salt and pepper to taste
4 slices bacon, crisp-cooked, crumbled

SWEAT the carrot, onion and celery in the melted margarine in a saucepan over low heat until tender. ADD the flour. COOK for 1 minute, stirring constantly. STIR in the chicken stock. BRING to a boil and reduce the heat. SIMMER for 5 minutes or until thickened, stirring constantly. STIR in the cream. ADD the cheese just before serving, stirring until the cheese melts. SEASON with Worcestershire sauce, salt and pepper. TOP servings with the bacon.

NOTE: Can add other vegetables such as cauliflower, potatoes or broccoli as desired, or substitute low-sodium stock, low-fat cheese and half-and-half.

Cream of Chestnut Soup

YIELD: 4 TO 6 SERVINGS

1 large onion, chopped
2 tablespoons butter
1 (10-ounce) can chestnuts, drained,
    or vacuum-pack chestnuts
1 large carrot, chopped
2 cups chicken stock

1 chicken bouillon cube
3/4 cup light cream
1/4 cup sherry
Salt and pepper to taste
Whipped cream

SAUTÉ the onion in the butter in a saucepan until light brown. ADD the chestnuts, carrot, chicken stock and bouillon cube. SIMMER for 20 minutes. POUR into a food processor container and process until smooth. COMBINE with the cream and sherry in the saucepan and mix well. SEASON with salt and pepper. COOK just until heated through; do not boil. GARNISH servings with whipped cream.

Lentil Chili

YIELD: 8 TO 10 SERVINGS

1 pound dried lentils
1 onion, chopped
1 pound ground turkey
10 cups water
1 (29-ounce) can crushed tomatoes

2 cups salsa
1 teaspoon cumin
1 teaspoon chili powder
2 teaspoons salt
Shredded Cheddar cheese

SORT and rinse the lentils; drain. SPRAY a stockpot with nonstick cooking spray. ADD the onion. COOK over low heat for 5 minutes, stirring frequently. CRUMBLE the turkey into the stockpot. COOK until the turkey is opaque, stirring constantly. ADD the lentils and water and reduce the heat to low. SIMMER for 1 1/2 hours. ADD the tomatoes, salsa, cumin, chili powder and salt. SIMMER for 15 minutes. GARNISH servings with shredded Cheddar cheese.

Entrées

ENCHANTED EVENINGS

MENU

PESTO TORTE WITH GARLIC TOASTS – PAGE 37

STRAWBERRY SPINACH SALAD WITH POPPY SEED DRESSING – PAGE 54

GRILLED GARLIC LAMB CHOPS – PAGE 73

GREEN BEANS PROVENÇAL – PAGE 109

LEMON RICE – PAGE 116

HERBED SPOON ROLLS – PAGE 129

FUDGE TRUFFLE CHEESECAKE – PAGE 138

Beef Tenderloin with Médoc Sauce

YIELD: 10 SERVINGS

6 pounds beef tenderloin (usually
  2 short tenderloins)

2 to 3 tablespoons melted butter
Médoc Sauce

TRIM the tenderloin to make an even circumference. TIE with butcher's twine at 1½-inch intervals. PLACE on a rack in a roasting pan. BRUSH with melted butter. BAKE at 400 degrees for 35 to 45 minutes or until of the desired degree of doneness, turning every 7 or 8 minutes and basting with melted butter. LET stand for 10 to 15 minutes before slicing. SERVE with the Médoc Sauce.

NOTE: The tenderloin is rare at an internal temperature of 120 degrees. The tenderloin can also be grilled.

MÉDOC SAUCE

8 cups water
6 bouillon cubes
2 cups Médoc or other burgundy
½ cup tomato purée
1 cup finely chopped mushrooms
2 tablespoons butter

½ cup each minced celery, carrot
  and onion
5 to 6 tablespoons melted butter
6 tablespoons flour
1 tablespoon lemon juice
1 tablespoon chopped parsley

MIX the water, bouillon cubes, wine and tomato purée in a large saucepan. SIMMER over medium heat for 2½ hours or until reduced to 5 cups. SAUTÉ the mushrooms in 2 tablespoons butter in a skillet until brown. SAUTÉ the celery, carrot and onion in 3 tablespoons of the melted butter in a skillet over low heat for 20 minutes or until the vegetables are tender. DRAIN, reserving the pan drippings. ADD the vegetables to the sauce. SIMMER over low heat for 15 minutes. STRAIN to remove the vegetables. COMBINE the reserved pan drippings with enough of the remaining melted butter to measure 6 tablespoons and place in a skillet. HEAT over medium-low heat. WHISK in the flour 1 tablespoon at a time, stirring constantly. ADD the sauce gradually. SIMMER until thickened, stirring constantly. ADD the sautéed mushrooms, lemon juice and parsley. ADD additional wine if needed to make of the desired consistency.

Spicy Marinated Flank Steak

YIELD: 8 TO 10 SERVINGS

2 flank steaks
1 1/2 cups vegetable oil
3/4 cup soy sauce
1/2 cup wine vinegar
1/3 cup lemon juice

1/4 cup Worcestershire sauce
2 tablespoons dry mustard
2 teaspoons salt
1 teaspoon pepper
2 or 3 garlic cloves, crushed

SCORE the steaks in a diamond pattern with a sharp knife. PLACE in a deep dish. COMBINE the vegetable oil, soy sauce, wine vinegar, lemon juice, Worcestershire sauce, dry mustard, salt and pepper in a bowl and mix well. POUR over the steaks. MARINATE, covered, in the refrigerator for 8 hours or longer. DRAIN the steaks, discarding the marinade. PLACE on a grill rack. GRILL over hot coals until of the desired degree of doneness. CUT the steaks across the grain into thin slices to serve.

Grilled London Broil with Red Wine Marinade

YIELD: 4 TO 6 SERVINGS

2 to 3 pounds London broil
2 to 3 onions
1/2 cup vegetable oil

1/2 cup dry red wine
1/2 cup low-sodium soy sauce

PLACE the beef in a shallow glass dish. CUT the onions into slices and separate into rings. PLACE the onion rings over the beef. MIX the vegetable oil, red wine and soy sauce in a bowl. POUR over the onion rings and beef. MARINATE, covered, in the refrigerator for 3 to 5 hours, turning frequently. DRAIN the beef, reserving the marinade. BRING the reserved marinade to a boil in a saucepan. BOIL for 2 to 3 minutes. REMOVE from the heat. PLACE the beef on a grill rack. GRILL over hot coals until of the desired degree of doneness. CUT the beef diagonally into thin slices. SPOON the boiled reserved marinade over the beef to serve.

Spicy Sesame Teriyaki Shish Kabobs

YIELD: VARIABLE

4 ounces beef, 4 ounces lamb, 1 to 2 chicken breast halves or $1/2$ to 1 salmon steak per person

Sesame Teriyaki Glaze

CUT the beef, lamb, chicken or salmon into $1^1/_2$-inch pieces. PLACE each in separate sealable plastic bags if grilling a variety. ADD the Sesame Teriyaki Glaze to each bag. MARINATE in the refrigerator for up to 1 hour, turning several times. DRAIN, reserving the Sesame Teriyaki Glaze. BRING the reserved Sesame Teriyaki Glaze to a boil in a saucepan. BOIL for 2 to 3 minutes. REMOVE from the heat. THREAD 4 or 5 pieces of beef, lamb, chicken or salmon onto each skewer. GRILL over hot coals until of the desired degree of doneness. THE beef or lamb will need to be grilled 5 to 6 minutes per side; the chicken will need to be grilled 4 to 5 minutes per side or until cooked through; and the salmon will need to be grilled 3 to 4 minutes per side or until the salmon flakes easily. SERVE with the boiled Sesame Teriyaki Glaze.

SESAME TERIYAKI GLAZE

$1/2$ cup unsweetened pineapple juice
$1/2$ cup soy sauce
$1/2$ cup sherry
$1/4$ cup packed brown sugar
1 tablespoon plus 1 teaspoon cornstarch

$1^1/_2$ teaspoons grated fresh gingerroot
2 garlic cloves
1 tablespoon sesame seeds

COMBINE the pineapple juice, soy sauce, sherry, brown sugar, cornstarch, gingerroot, garlic and sesame seeds in a medium saucepan. BRING to a boil over high heat. REDUCE the heat to medium. COOK for 2 to 3 minutes or until thickened, stirring constantly. COOL completely before using as a marinade.

Teriyaki Hamburgers

YIELD: 4 SERVINGS

1 pound lean ground beef
^{1}/$_3$ cup chopped water chestnuts
^{1}/$_4$ cup chopped green bell peppers
2 green onions, finely chopped
2 tablespoons water
1 tablespoon brown sugar

1 tablespoon lemon juice
1 tablespoon soy sauce
^{1}/$_2$ teaspoon minced fresh gingerroot
4 sesame seed buns, split
Hoisin Catsup

COMBINE the ground beef, water chestnuts, green peppers, green onions, water, brown sugar, lemon juice, soy sauce and gingerroot in a bowl and mix well. SHAPE into 4 patties. PLACE on a plate and cover with plastic wrap. FREEZE for 10 to 15 minutes. UNCOVER the patties. PLACE on a grill rack sprayed with nonstick cooking spray. GRILL over medium-hot coals for 5 minutes per side or until cooked through. PLACE the patties on the bottom halves of the buns. SPREAD with the Hoisin Catsup. TOP with the remaining bun halves.

HOISIN CATSUP

^{1}/$_4$ cup catsup

^{1}/$_4$ cup hoisin sauce

COMBINE the catsup and hoisin sauce in a bowl and mix well. STORE in an air-tight container in the refrigerator until ready to serve.

Fiesta Pork

YIELD: 4 SERVINGS

1 pound boneless pork loin, cubed
1 tablespoon taco seasoning mix
2 teaspoons vegetable oil

1 (8-ounce) jar salsa
1/3 cup peach or apple jelly

PLACE the pork and taco seasoning mix in a sealable plastic bag. SEAL the bag and shake until the pork is coated. HEAT the vegetable oil in a skillet over medium-high heat. ADD the pork. COOK until the pork is brown. ADD the salsa. SIMMER, covered, for 15 to 20 minutes or until the pork is tender and cooked through. ADD the jelly. COOK until heated through. SERVE with cooked rice or tortillas.

Jamaican Pork Tenderloin

YIELD: 2 TO 4 SERVINGS

1 (1-pound) lean pork tenderloin
3 tablespoons lime juice
1 tablespoon chopped jalapeño
1 teaspoon chopped fresh gingerroot
   (optional)

1/4 teaspoon salt
1/4 teaspoon ground allspice

PLACE the pork in a large sealable plastic bag. COMBINE the lime juice, jalapeño, gingerroot, salt and allspice in a bowl and mix well. POUR over the pork and seal the bag. MARINATE in the refrigerator for 30 minutes or up to 12 hours. DRAIN the pork, reserving the marinade. BOIL the reserved marinade in a saucepan for 2 to 3 minutes. REMOVE from the heat. PLACE the pork on an oiled grill rack. GRILL over hot coals for 27 minutes or until a meat thermometer registers 160 degrees when inserted into the thickest part, turning occasionally and basting with the boiled reserved marinade.

*Medallions of
Pork with Prunes*

YIELD: 4 SERVINGS

8 slices boneless pork tenderloin,
    trimmed (about 3 ounces each)
2 teaspoons ground cumin
Salt and freshly ground pepper to
    taste
2 tablespoons vegetable oil
2 sprigs of fresh rosemary, or
    1 teaspoon dried rosemary
$1/2$ cup finely chopped onion

1 teaspoon chopped garlic
$1/4$ cup port
1 tablespoon red wine vinegar
1 tablespoon tomato paste
$1/2$ cup fresh or canned chicken broth
24 pitted prunes
2 tablespoons butter
2 tablespoons finely chopped fresh
    coriander or parsley

PLACE the pork in a shallow glass dish. SEASON with a mixture of cumin, salt
and pepper. HEAT the vegetable oil in a large nonstick skillet. ARRANGE the pork
in 1 layer in the skillet and add the rosemary. COOK over medium heat for 5
minutes or until brown. TURN over the pork. COOK for 5 minutes longer.
REDUCE the heat. CONTINUE cooking for a few minutes longer or until cooked
through. REMOVE the pork to a warm platter and discard the pan drippings.
ADD the onion and garlic to the skillet. SAUTÉ until the onion is wilted. ADD the
wine, red wine vinegar, tomato paste and chicken broth, stirring to deglaze the
skillet. ADD the prunes. COOK until the mixture is reduced by half. RETURN the
pork and any accumulated juices to the skillet. ADD the butter. BRING to a simmer, shaking the skillet to blend in the butter. SPRINKLE with the coriander.
SERVE immediately.

Grilled Spiced Pork Tenderloins with Dried Cherry Chutney

YIELD: 8 SERVINGS

2 tablespoons paprika
1 tablespoon chili powder
1 teaspoon cumin
1 teaspoon ground coriander
1 teaspoon salt
1/2 teaspoon dry mustard

1/2 teaspoon ground black pepper
1/2 teaspoon thyme
1/2 teaspoon curry powder
1/2 teaspoon cayenne
4 pork tenderloins
Dried Cherry Chutney

COMBINE the paprika, chili powder, cumin, coriander, salt, dry mustard, black pepper, thyme, curry powder and cayenne in a bowl and mix well. RUB on the pork. PLACE on an oiled grill rack. GRILL over hot coals for 20 minutes or until a meat thermometer registers 150 degrees when inserted in the thickest portion, turning frequently. LET stand for 5 minutes before slicing. SERVE with the Dried Cherry Chutney.

NOTE: Mix up extra spice rub and store in an airtight container. Use also to rub on chicken breast halves before grilling.

DRIED CHERRY CHUTNEY

2 1/2 cups sugar
1 1/2 cups cider vinegar
1 cup apple cider
1/2 cup chopped fresh gingerroot

2 Granny Smith apples, peeled, chopped
1 quart dried cherries
1 teaspoon crushed red pepper

COMBINE the sugar, cider vinegar and apple cider in a saucepan. COOK over low heat until the sugar dissolves, stirring constantly. ADD the gingerroot, apples, dried cherries and red pepper. SIMMER over low heat for 30 minutes or until thickened and nearly all the liquid has been absorbed. LET stand until cool before serving.

Embers Pork Chops

YIELD: 6 SERVINGS

2 cups soy sauce
1 cup water
1/2 cup packed brown sugar
1 tablespoon molasses

1 teaspoon salt
6 pork chops with bone in
   (1 1/2 to 2 inches thick)
Red Sauce

BRING the soy sauce, water, brown sugar, molasses and salt to a boil in a saucepan over medium heat. COOK for 3 to 4 minutes, stirring frequently. REMOVE from the heat. PLACE the pork chops in a large baking pan with the bone side up. POUR the marinade over the pork chops. MARINATE, covered, in the refrigerator for 10 to 12 hours, turning several times. REMOVE the pork chops from the marinade. POUR the marinade into a saucepan. BRING to a boil. BOIL for 2 to 3 minutes, stirring frequently. STRAIN the marinade into a freezer container. LET stand until cool. FREEZE for later use. RETURN the pork chops to the baking pan and cover tightly with foil. BAKE at 375 degrees for 1 1/2 hours. REDUCE the oven temperature to 350 degrees. REMOVE the pork chops from the oven. DIP each pork chop into the Red Sauce and return to the baking pan. COOK, uncovered, for 20 to 30 minutes or until slightly glazed, or grill the pork chops for 15 to 20 minutes or until glazed. SERVE with the remaining Red Sauce.

RED SAUCE

1 (14-ounce) bottle catsup
1 (12-ounce) bottle chili sauce
1/3 cup water

1/2 cup packed brown sugar
1 tablespoon dry mustard

COMBINE the catsup, chili sauce, water, brown sugar and dry mustard in a saucepan and mix well. BRING to a boil, stirring frequently. REMOVE from the heat.

Ham and Cheese Picnic Pie

YIELD: 12 TO 15 SERVINGS

1 recipe (2-crust) pie pastry
3 eggs
1 (15-ounce) container ricotta cheese
1 (15-ounce) container small curd
   cottage cheese, drained
1/2 cup seasoned bread crumbs
1/2 cup grated Parmesan cheese
1/4 cup minced fresh parsley
1 1/2 teaspoons Creole or Italian
   seasoning

Salt to taste
1/2 to 1 teaspoon freshly ground
   pepper
2 or 3 dashes hot sauce
1 pound deli ham, cut into
   1/4-inch cubes
4 ounces mozzarella cheese, cut into
   1/4-inch cubes
1 bunch green onions, thinly sliced
1 egg, beaten

ROLL half the pastry into an 11-inch circle. FIT into a 10-inch springform pan. CHILL in the refrigerator. BEAT 3 eggs in a large bowl. ADD the ricotta cheese, cottage cheese, bread crumbs, Parmesan cheese, parsley, 1 teaspoon of the Creole seasoning, salt, pepper and hot sauce and mix well. STIR in the ham, mozzarella cheese and green onions. POUR into the pastry-lined pan. PULL the edge of the pastry over the filling. BRUSH with 1/2 of the beaten egg. ROLL the remaining pastry into a 12-inch circle. PLACE over the filling, crimping the edges of the pastry together; the edge will be inside the springform pan. BRUSH with the remaining beaten egg. SPRINKLE with the remaining 1/2 teaspoon Creole seasoning. BAKE at 375 degrees for 1 hour and 10 minutes. REMOVE from the oven. LET stand until cool. CHILL in the refrigerator. SERVE at room temperature.

Greek Lamb Shanks

YIELD: 4 SERVINGS

1/2 cup flour
1/2 teaspoon seasoned salt
4 meaty lamb shanks
2 tablespoons olive oil
1 envelope chili seasoning mix with
  onions

1/4 cup grated Parmesan cheese
1 (10-ounce) can tomato soup
1 (28-ounce) can crushed tomatoes

MIX the flour and seasoned salt in a large sealable plastic bag. ADD the lamb shanks. SEAL the bag and shake until the lamb shanks are coated with the flour mixture. HEAT the olive oil in a large roasting pan on top of the stove. ADD the lamb shanks. COOK until brown on all sides. SPRINKLE with the seasoning mix and Parmesan cheese. POUR the soup and tomatoes over the top. BAKE, covered, at 250 degrees for 6 to 8 hours or until cooked through. SERVE with cooked green beans or white beans.

Grilled Garlic Lamb Chops

YIELD: 6 SERVINGS

6 (1-inch-thick) lamb sirloin chops,
  trimmed
1/2 cup soy sauce
1/2 cup cider vinegar
3 garlic cloves, minced

3 tablespoons honey
2 teaspoons ground ginger
1/4 teaspoon dry mustard
1/4 teaspoon freshly ground pepper

PLACE the lamb chops in a sealable plastic bag. COMBINE the soy sauce, cider vinegar, garlic, honey, ginger, dry mustard and pepper in a bowl and mix well. POUR over the lamb chops and seal the bag. MARINATE in the refrigerator for 8 hours or longer, turning several times. DRAIN the lamb chops, reserving the marinade. BOIL the marinade in a saucepan for 2 to 3 minutes. REMOVE from the heat. PLACE the lamb chops on a grill rack. GRILL over medium coals for 8 to 10 minutes per side or to the desired degree of doneness, basting with the boiled reserved marinade.

Creamy Almond Chicken

YIELD: 6 SERVINGS

$^2/_3$ cup sliced almonds
4 tablespoons butter
6 boneless skinless chicken breast
   halves
Salt and black pepper to taste

$1^1/_2$ cups heavy cream
1 tablespoon Dijon mustard
2 tablespoons orange marmalade
$^1/_8$ teaspoon red pepper

SAUTÉ the almonds in 1 tablespoon of the butter in a skillet until light brown. PLACE the chicken between sheets of plastic wrap and pound $^1/_4$ inch thick. SEASON with salt and black pepper. HEAT the remaining 3 tablespoons butter in a skillet over medium-high heat. ADD the chicken. COOK until golden brown, turning frequently. REDUCE the heat to medium. ADD $^1/_2$ cup of the almonds, cream, Dijon mustard, marmalade and red pepper. COOK for 10 minutes longer or until the chicken is cooked through and the sauce is thickened, stirring constantly. SERVE over rice and sprinkle with the remaining almonds.

Baked Apricot Chicken

YIELD: 4 SERVINGS

1 ($2^1/_2$-pound) chicken, cut up
1 cup apricot preserves
$^1/_4$ bottle Russian salad dressing

2 tablespoons mayonnaise or
   mayonnaise-type salad dressing
$^1/_2$ envelope onion soup mix

ARRANGE the chicken in a 2-quart baking dish. COMBINE the preserves, salad dressing, mayonnaise and soup mix in a bowl and mix well. SPREAD over the chicken. BAKE at 350 degrees for 1 hour or until the chicken is cooked through and tender.

NOTE: Boneless chicken breasts can be substituted for the whole chicken.

Cranberry Chicken

YIELD: 4 TO 6 SERVINGS

4 to 6 boneless skinless chicken breast halves
1 envelope onion soup mix
1 bottle Catalina salad dressing
1 (16-ounce) can whole cranberry sauce

PLACE the chicken in a lightly greased 9x13-inch baking dish. COMBINE the soup mix, salad dressing and cranberry sauce in a bowl and mix well. POUR over the chicken. MARINATE, covered, in the refrigerator for 6 to 12 hours. BAKE, uncovered, at 350 degrees for 1 hour or until the chicken is cooked through. SERVE with rice.

Hawaiian Chicken

YIELD: 4 SERVINGS

1 (6-ounce) can pineapple juice
$^1\!/_2$ cup soy sauce
3 tablespoons brown sugar
$^1\!/_2$ teaspoon freshly grated gingerroot
1 garlic clove, crushed
2 tablespoons sherry
4 boneless skinless chicken breast halves

COMBINE the pineapple juice, soy sauce, brown sugar, gingerroot, garlic and sherry in a bowl and mix well. POUR over the chicken in a sealable plastic bag. SEAL the bag and shake well to coat. MARINATE in the refrigerator for 30 to 60 minutes. DRAIN the chicken, discarding the marinade. PLACE the chicken on a grill rack. GRILL over hot coals for 10 to 15 minutes or until cooked through.

Kelton House
Chicken Divan

YIELD: 8 TO 10 SERVINGS

1 large onion
6 boneless chicken breast halves
Dried or fresh chopped herbs of
   choice to taste
Salt and freshly ground pepper
   to taste
1 (26-ounce) can cream of mushroom
   soup

3/4 soup can mayonnaise
1/2 teaspoon curry powder, or to taste
1 (family-size) package frozen broccoli
   cuts, thawed, drained
2 cups shredded sharp Cheddar
   cheese
1 (6-ounce) package cheese croutons
Chopped fresh parsley

CUT the onion into halves. CUT the onion halves into slices. PLACE the onion in a baking pan. ARRANGE the chicken in a single layer over the onion. SPRINKLE with herbs, salt and pepper. BAKE at 350 degrees for 15 minutes or until just barely cooked through. DO not overcook. COOL the chicken and tear into pieces. COMBINE the soup, mayonnaise and curry powder in a bowl and mix well. SPOON 2 to 3 tablespoons of the soup mixture in a buttered 9x13-inch baking dish. LAYER the broccoli, chicken and remaining soup mixture in the prepared dish. SPRINKLE 1/2 of the cheese over the layers. BAKE at 350 degrees for 20 minutes. SPRINKLE the croutons and remaining cheese over the top. BAKE for 10 minutes longer or until the sauce is bubbly. GARNISH with chopped parsley.

Lemon Chicken

YIELD: 8 SERVINGS

8 chicken breast halves
2 cups fresh lemon juice
2 cups flour
2 teaspoons paprika
2 teaspoons salt
1 teaspoon freshly ground pepper

¹/₂ cup vegetable oil
2 tablespoons grated lemon peel
¹/₄ cup packed brown sugar
¹/₄ cup chicken broth
2 tablespoons lemon juice
2 lemons, thinly sliced

PLACE the chicken in a bowl and add 2 cups lemon juice. MARINATE, covered, in the refrigerator for 6 hours, turning occasionally. DRAIN the chicken and pat dry, discarding the lemon juice. COMBINE the flour, paprika, salt and pepper in a small sealable plastic bag and shake to mix well. ADD the chicken 1 piece at a time and shake until coated completely with the flour mixture. HEAT the vegetable oil in a large skillet. ADD the chicken. FRY until light brown and crispy. PLACE the chicken in a shallow baking pan. SPRINKLE with the lemon peel and brown sugar. POUR a mixture of the chicken broth and 2 tablespoons lemon juice around the chicken. PLACE a thin lemon slice on each chicken piece. BAKE at 375 degrees for 35 to 40 minutes or until the chicken is cooked through.

Mexican Chicken

YIELD: 4 SERVINGS

4 boneless skinless chicken breast
  halves
1 envelope taco seasoning mix
2 green onions, sliced

¹/₄ cup sliced black olives
1 (15-ounce) can diced tomatoes
¹/₂ cup shredded Cheddar cheese
Sour cream

PLACE the chicken in a 9x13-inch baking dish. COMBINE the taco seasoning mix, green onions, black olives and tomatoes in a bowl and mix well. POUR over the chicken. SPRINKLE with the cheese. BAKE at 375 degrees for 45 to 60 minutes or until cooked through. GARNISH with sour cream.

Chicken Elizabeth

YIELD: 4 SERVINGS

8 ounces cream cheese, softened
1/2 cup margarine, softened
1 teaspoon minced garlic
1 teaspoon each basil, oregano, thyme, tarragon and parsley

1/8 teaspoon pepper
4 whole boneless chicken breasts
4 ounces ham, cut into very thin slices
12 cherry tomatoes, cut into halves
White wine

COMBINE the cream cheese, margarine, garlic, basil, oregano, thyme, tarragon, parsley and pepper in a bowl and mix well. PLACE the chicken between 2 sheets of plastic wrap and pound 1/2 inch thick. LINE each chicken breast with 1 ounce of ham, 6 tomato halves and 1/4 cup of the cream cheese mixture. ROLL up and secure with wooden picks or string. PLACE seam side down in a baking dish. TOP each chicken roll-up with a dollop of the remaining cream cheese mixture. SPRINKLE generously with wine. BAKE, covered, at 375 degrees for 20 minutes. BAKE, uncovered, for 10 minutes longer or until the chicken is cooked through.

Pecan Chicken

YIELD: 4 OR 5 SERVINGS

4 or 5 boneless skinless chicken breast halves
1 (8-ounce) bottle creamy Italian salad dressing

1/2 cup bread crumbs
1/2 cup crushed pecans
Butter or margarine

PLACE the chicken in a bowl and prick several times with a fork so that the marinade can be absorbed. ADD the salad dressing. MARINATE, covered, in the refrigerator for 3 to 8 hours. COMBINE the bread crumbs and pecans in a large sealable plastic bag and shake to mix well. ADD the chicken 1 piece at a time and shake until well coated. ARRANGE the chicken in a glass baking dish sprayed with nonstick cooking spray. BAKE at 350 degrees for 18 to 20 minutes. DOT each chicken piece with butter. BAKE for 18 to 20 minutes longer or until cooked through.

Pecan and Peanut Chicken Breasts with Pesto Sauce

YIELD: 6 SERVINGS

6 boneless skinless chicken breasts
3 tablespoons melted butter
1/4 cup grated Parmesan cheese
1 cup finely chopped peanuts
1/2 cup finely chopped pecans

1 cup light sour cream
1/3 cup pesto
3 tablespoons chopped fresh basil
1 tablespoon butter
1 tablespoon peanut oil

POUND the chicken between waxed paper until flat. BRUSH with 3 tablepoons butter. MIX the Parmesan cheese, peanuts and pecans on a plate. COAT the chicken with the peanut mixture. LET stand on waxed paper for 30 minutes. HEAT the sour cream and pesto in a small saucepan until heated through; do not simmer. STIR in the basil. MELT 1 tablespoon butter with the peanut oil in a large skillet. ADD the chicken. COOK for 3 to 4 minutes on each side or until the chicken is cooked through. SERVE with the pesto sauce.

Grilled Chicken Breasts with Orange Mint Pesto

YIELD: 6 SERVINGS

1/2 cup pecans
1 cup packed fresh basil leaves
1/2 cup packed fresh mint leaves
2 garlic cloves
2 tablespoons orange juice
  concentrate

1/3 to 1/2 cup olive oil
Salt and freshly ground pepper
  to taste
6 boneless chicken breast halves
1/3 cup heavy cream (optional)

ARRANGE the pecans in a single layer on a baking sheet. BAKE at 350 degrees for 8 to 10 minutes or until toasted. PROCESS the pecans, basil, mint, garlic and orange juice concentrate in a food processor until almost smooth. ADD the olive oil in a fine stream, processing constantly. SEASON with salt and pepper. PLACE the chicken in a bowl. ADD 3/4 of the pesto. MARINATE, covered, in the refrigerator for 30 to 40 minutes. DRAIN the chicken, discarding the marinade. PLACE on a grill rack. GRILL over low coals until cooked through, turning frequently. SERVE with a mixture of the remaining pesto and cream.

Grilled Plum Chicken

YIELD: 6 SERVINGS

6 boneless skinless chicken breast
  halves
3 tablespoons balsamic vinegar
2 tablespoons Dijon mustard

$^1/_2$ teaspoon sea salt
$^1/_4$ teaspoon coarsely ground pepper
$^1/_2$ cup plus 1 tablespoon olive oil
$^1/_3$ cup plum sauce

PLACE the chicken in a shallow non-aluminum dish. COMBINE the balsamic vinegar, Dijon mustard, sea salt and pepper in a bowl and whisk until blended. ADD the olive oil gradually, whisking constantly. POUR over the chicken. MARINATE, covered, in the refrigerator for 6 to 12 hours, turning several times. DRAIN the chicken, discarding the marinade. PLACE the chicken on a grill rack. GRILL over hot coals for 10 to 12 minutes or until cooked through. BRUSH the chicken with the plum sauce. GRILL for 1 minute longer.

Chicken with Honey

YIELD: 4 TO 6 SERVINGS

$^1/_2$ cup honey
$^1/_4$ cup prepared mustard
3 tablespoons milk
3 tablespoons melted butter

1 teaspoon curry powder
1 teaspoon salt
6 to 8 chicken pieces

COMBINE the honey, mustard, milk, butter, curry powder and salt in a bowl and mix well. ROLL each chicken piece in the honey mixture until coated and place in a baking dish. POUR any remaining honey mixture over the chicken. BAKE at 350 degrees for 1 to $1^1/_4$ hours or until cooked through, basting frequently with the honey mixture.

Chicken Chimichangas

YIELD: 4 SERVINGS

2¹/₂ cups shredded cooked chicken
(about 5 chicken breast halves)
²/₃ cup salsa
2 green onions, sliced
1 teaspoon cumin
¹/₂ teaspoon oregano
¹/₂ teaspoon salt, or to taste
8 (7- or 8-inch) flour tortillas
¹/₄ cup melted butter or margarine
1 cup shredded Cheddar or Monterey Jack cheese

COMBINE the chicken, salsa, green onions, cumin, oregano and salt in a saucepan. BRING to a boil and reduce the heat. SIMMER for 5 minutes or until most of the liquid has evaporated. BRUSH 1 side of each tortilla with butter. SPOON about ¹/₃ cup of the chicken mixture in the center of the unbuttered side of 1 tortilla. SPRINKLE with 2 tablespoons of the cheese. FOLD 1 end of the tortilla up. FOLD the sides over and the top down. PLACE seam side down on a baking sheet with sides sprayed with nonstick cooking spray. REPEAT with the remaining tortillas, chicken mixture and cheese. BAKE at 475 degrees for 13 minutes or until crisp and golden brown.

NOTE: Chimichangas can be refrigerated before baking. Bake at 325 degrees for 10 minutes. Increase the oven temperature to 475 degrees. Bake for 10 to 12 minutes longer or until golden brown.

Pollo Tonnato

YIELD: 4 TO 6 SERVINGS

3 tablespoons olive oil
1 carrot, sliced
1 rib celery, thinly sliced
1/2 medium onion, sliced
1/2 cup dry white wine
6 boneless skinless chicken breast halves
1 (7-ounce) can oil-pack tuna, drained
5 canned flat anchovies
3 tablespoons lemon juice
3 tablespoons drained capers
1 1/4 cups olive oil
1 cup mayonnaise
Capers
Lemon slices

HEAT 3 tablespoons olive oil in a large skillet. ADD the carrot, celery and onion. COOK, covered, over low heat for 10 minutes or until the vegetables are wilted. ADD the wine. COOK for 2 minutes. ADD the chicken. COOK, covered, for 10 to 15 minutes or until the chicken is cooked through. REMOVE from the heat. LET stand until cool. COMBINE the tuna, anchovies, lemon juice and 3 table-spoons capers in a food processor container. ADD 1 1/4 cups olive oil gradually, processing until of a creamy consistency. FOLD into the mayonnaise in a bowl. CUT the cooled chicken into 1/4-inch-thick scallops. SPREAD some of the tuna sauce on a platter. LAYER the chicken scallops on the prepared platter, spreading additional tuna sauce between each chicken layer. COVER with the remaining tuna sauce, smoothing the surface with a spatula. WRAP tightly in plastic wrap. CHILL in the refrigerator until serving time. GARNISH with additional capers and thin lemon slices.

Grilled Grouper

YIELD: 4 SERVINGS

1 tablespoon minced onion
1 1/2 teaspoons grated Parmesan
    cheese or Romano cheese
3/4 teaspoon sugar
2 teaspoons salt or Mrs. Dash
    seasoning
3/4 teaspoon ground pepper

3/4 teaspoon basil
3/4 teaspoon dry mustard
3/4 teaspoon oregano
1/4 cup red wine
1 tablespoon lemon juice
1/2 cup olive oil
2 pounds grouper fillets

COMBINE the onion, Parmesan cheese, sugar, salt, pepper, basil, dry mustard, oregano, wine and lemon juice in a blender container and process well. ADD the olive oil in a steady stream, processing constantly at high speed. SPRAY the fish fillets with nonstick cooking spray. DIP each fillet in the sauce. PLACE on a grill rack sprayed with nonstick cooking spray. BRING the remaining sauce to a boil in a saucepan. BOIL for 2 to 3 minutes. REMOVE from the heat. GRILL the fish fillets for 10 minutes on each side or until the fish fillets flake easily, basting with the cooked sauce.

NOTE: Can substitute 1/2 tablespoon lime juice for 1/2 of the lemon juice.

Herb and Garlic Fish

YIELD: 4 SERVINGS

1/2 cup mayonnaise or mayonnaise-
    type salad dressing
1/2 teaspoon dried marjoram leaves
1/2 teaspoon dried thyme leaves

1/2 teaspoon garlic powder
1/4 teaspoon ground celery seed
1 pound grouper, flounder, mahimahi
    or swordfish fillets

COMBINE the mayonnaise, marjoram, thyme, garlic powder and celery seed in a bowl and mix well. PLACE the fish on an oiled grill rack. BRUSH with 1/2 of the mayonnaise mixture. GRILL over medium-hot coals for 5 to 8 minutes. TURN over the fish. BRUSH with the remaining mayonnaise mixture. GRILL for 5 to 8 minutes longer or until the fish flakes easily with a fork.

Grilled Salmon Steaks with Sun-Dried Tomato Sauce

YIELD: 4 SERVINGS

2/3 cup sun-dried tomatoes
1 cup water
1/8 teaspoon cayenne
2 tablespoons catsup
2 tablespoons tomato paste
1 1/2 teaspoons minced drained capers
2 teaspoons balsamic vinegar
1/2 teaspoon minced fresh parsley
1/2 teaspoon dried tarragon
1 tablespoon minced fresh chives
1/2 teaspoon freshly ground black pepper
2 tablespoons fresh lemon juice
1/2 teaspoon minced garlic
1/4 teaspoon salt
2 tablespoons cider vinegar
1/4 cup vegetable oil
1 cup water
4 (8-ounce) salmon steaks, 1 inch thick

SIMMER sun-dried tomatoes in 1 cup water in a small saucepan for 3 minutes. LET stand until cool. DRAIN, reserving the liquid. CHOP the tomatoes finely and place in a bowl. ADD the reserved liquid, cayenne, catsup, tomato paste, capers, balsamic vinegar, parsley, tarragon, chives, black pepper, lemon juice, garlic, salt, cider vinegar, vegetable oil and 1/2 cup of the remaining water and mix well. COVER and let stand for 2 to 12 hours. COMBINE 1/2 of the sun-dried tomato sauce and the remaining water in a large shallow glass dish. ADD the salmon, turning to coat well. MARINATE, covered, in the refrigerator for 2 hours. DRAIN the salmon, reserving the marinade. BRING the reserved marinade to a boil in a small saucepan. BOIL for 2 to 3 minutes and remove from the heat. PLACE the salmon on a grill rack. GRILL 4 inches from the hot coals for 13 to 15 minutes or until the salmon flakes easily, brushing frequently with the cooked marinade and turning once. SERVE with the remaining sun-dried tomato sauce.

Crabmeat Cakes

YIELD: 4 SERVINGS

1 pound backfin crabmeat
1 egg
2 tablespoons mayonnaise
1 tablespoon prepared horseradish
 mustard
1 tablespoon chopped fresh parsley

$^1/_4$ teaspoon salt or Mrs. Dash
 seasoning
$^1/_8$ teaspoon ground pepper
1 package saltine crackers, crumbled
Vegetable oil for frying

COMBINE the crabmeat, egg, mayonnaise, mustard, parsley, salt and pepper in a bowl and mix well. SHAPE into patties. COAT each patty with cracker crumbs. FRY the patties in hot vegetable oil until golden brown, turning once.

Cashew Shrimp

YIELD: 4 SERVINGS

1 pound shrimp
3 tablespoons sherry
1$^1/_4$ teaspoons minced gingerroot
3 tablespoons vegetable oil
$^1/_3$ cup cashews
2 tablespoons mushrooms

$^1/_2$ cup sliced water chestnuts
1 teaspoon cornstarch
3 tablespoons soy sauce
$^1/_4$ teaspoon sugar
$^1/_4$ cup chopped scallions
$^1/_2$ teaspoon Oriental sesame oil

COMBINE the shrimp, 1 tablespoon of the sherry and gingerroot in a bowl and mix well. MARINATE, covered, in the refrigerator for 30 minutes. DRAIN the shrimp, discarding the marinade. HEAT the vegetable oil in a wok. ADD the cashews. STIR-FRY for 20 seconds and place in a dish. ADD the mushrooms, water chestnuts and shrimp to the wok. STIR-FRY for 1 minute. ADD a mixture of the remaining sherry, cornstarch, soy sauce and sugar. STIR-FRY until the sauce is thickened. REMOVE from the heat. STIR in the cashews, scallions and sesame oil. SERVE over cooked white rice.

Broccoli and Shrimp Stir-Fry

YIELD: 4 SERVINGS

1 tablespoon vegetable oil
12 ounces peeled deveined shrimp
2 cups fresh or frozen broccoli
1 medium red bell pepper, cut into thin 2-inch strips
$1/2$ cup snow peas
$1/2$ cup sliced fresh mushrooms
$1/4$ cup sliced water chestnuts
2 teaspoons instant chicken bouillon
$1/2$ cup boiling water
1 tablespoon cornstarch
1 teaspoon lemon juice
1 teaspoon dried basil leaves
$1/2$ cup cold water
$1/2$ cup sliced green onions

HEAT the vegetable oil in a wok over medium heat. ADD the shrimp. STIR-FRY for 4 minutes or until the shrimp turn pink. REMOVE the shrimp to a heated dish. ADD the broccoli, red pepper, snow peas, mushrooms and water chestnuts to the wok. STIR-FRY until the vegetables are tender-crisp. DISSOLVE the instant bouillon in the boiling water. STIR the cornstarch, lemon juice and basil into the cold water. ADD the bouillon mixture and cornstarch mixture to the vegetables. COOK until thickened, stirring constantly. ADD the green onions and shrimp. STIR-FRY until heated through. SERVE over cooked rice.

Curried Shrimp and Wild Rice

YIELD: 4 SERVINGS

¹/₄ cup butter
¹/₄ cup flour
¹/₂ teaspoon salt
¹/₈ teaspoon ground pepper
Paprika to taste
¹/₂ teaspoon to 1 tablespoon curry
   powder, or to taste

1¹/₂ cups milk
3 tablespoons sherry
1 pound shrimp, peeled, deveined,
   cooked
1 (6-ounce) package wild rice

MELT the butter in a skillet. ADD the flour, salt, pepper, paprika and curry powder and mix well. STIR in the milk gradually. COOK until thickened, stirring constantly. STIR in the sherry and shrimp. COOK the wild rice using package directions, discarding the seasoning packet. SERVE the shrimp mixture over the wild rice.

Marinated Shrimp

YIELD: 8 SERVINGS

1¹/₂ cups vegetable oil
³/₄ cup white vinegar
3 tablespoons drained capers
2¹/₂ teaspoons celery seeds
1¹/₂ teaspoons salt

Few drops of Tabasco sauce
2 cups minced white onions
2¹/₂ pounds shrimp, peeled, deveined,
   cooked

WHISK the vegetable oil and white vinegar in a bowl. ADD the capers, celery seeds, salt and Tabasco sauce and whisk well. STIR in the onions and shrimp. MARINATE, covered, in the refrigerator for 8 to 12 hours. SERVE with a fresh salad and bread to soak up the marinade.

Pasta

A SPECIAL GATHERING

MENU

GREEN SALAD WITH JICAMA AND ORANGE POPPY SEED DRESSING – PAGE 53

MOM'S BEST MANICOTTI – PAGE 91

CHEESE POPOVERS – PAGE 134

MOCHA CHOCOLATE TORTE – PAGE 152

FRANKLIN PARK CONSERVATORY AND BOTANICAL GARDENS

A Columbus landmark listed on the National Register of Historical Places, the Franklin Park Conservatory and Botanical Gardens preserves and enhances horticultural appreciation and environmental awareness. Visitors can not only appreciate their favorite flowers but also can see other plant species from around the world. The Conservatory, which dates to 1895, celebrates different events and exhibits year-round.

Sausage and Pepperoni Lasagna

YIELD: 6 SERVINGS

6 ounces ground pork or Italian sausage, crumbled
1 cup chopped onion
1 garlic clove, minced
1 tablespoon olive oil
1 (14-ounce) jar pizza sauce

$^3/_4$ cup sliced mushrooms
$^1/_2$ cup chopped pepperoni
1 teaspoon dried oregano
6 lasagna noodles, cooked, drained
1 cup shredded mozzarella cheese
$^1/_4$ cup grated Parmesan cheese

SAUTÉ the pork, onion and garlic in olive oil in a large skillet until the pork is cooked through; drain. STIR in the pizza sauce, mushrooms, pepperoni and oregano. BRING just to a boil and reduce the heat. SIMMER, covered, for 15 minutes, stirring occasionally. ARRANGE $^1/_2$ of the noodles in a greased 9x13-inch baking dish. LAYER $^1/_2$ of the sauce, mozzarella cheese, remaining noodles and remaining sauce in the prepared dish. SPRINKLE with the Parmesan cheese. BAKE at 375 degrees for 30 to 35 minutes or until heated through.

Spicy Valentine Fettuccini

YIELD: 6 SERVINGS

1$^1/_2$ pounds chorizo
Olive oil
2 onions, sliced
2 tablespoons chopped garlic
4 red bell peppers, cut into strips

20 sun-dried tomatoes, thinly sliced
$^1/_4$ cup red wine
2 cups heavy cream
1$^1/_2$ pounds fettuccini, cooked, drained

REMOVE the sausage from the casings and crumble into a large skillet. SAUTÉ until cooked through. REMOVE from the skillet. ADD enough olive oil to the skillet to just coat the bottom of the skillet. HEAT until the olive oil is smoking. ADD the onions and garlic. SAUTÉ over low heat until almost softened. ADD the red peppers and tomatoes. SAUTÉ for 3 minutes. ADD the wine. COOK until bubbly. ADD the cream. COOK for 5 minutes or until thickened, stirring constantly. RETURN the drained sausage to the skillet. COOK until heated through. ADD to the fettuccini in a large serving bowl and toss to mix well.

Mom's Best
Manicotti

YIELD: 8 TO 10 SERVINGS

2 garlic cloves, chopped
2 tablespoons olive oil
8 ounces boneless pork, cut into
    1-inch pieces
1 (28-ounce) can crushed tomatoes
1 cup water
1 teaspoon dried basil
1/4 teaspoon salt
3/4 teaspoon pepper
4 eggs

1 cup flour
1 cup water
1 cup ricotta cheese
1 cup small curd cottage cheese
1/4 cup grated Parmesan cheese
1 tablespoon chopped fresh parsley
1/4 teaspoon salt
1/4 teaspoon pepper
1 cup shredded mozzarella cheese

SAUTÉ the garlic in the olive oil for 1 to 2 minutes. ADD the pork. SAUTÉ until brown. STIR in the tomatoes, water, basil, 1/4 teaspoon salt and 3/4 teaspoon pepper. SIMMER for 2 to 3 hours. USE immediately or chill until ready to use. COMBINE the eggs, flour and water in a large bowl and whisk well. COAT the bottom of a 6- or 8-inch sauté pan with nonstick cooking spray and heat the pan. POUR in 1/4 cup of the batter and tilt the pan to form a 6-inch crepe. COOK until set, turning once if necessary. THE crepes can be filled immediately or chilled with waxed paper between each crepe to prevent sticking. COMBINE the ricotta cheese, cottage cheese, Parmesan cheese, parsley, 1/4 teaspoon salt and 1/4 teaspoon pepper in a bowl and mix well. USE immediately or cover and chill. POUR 2/3 cup of the tomato sauce into a 9-inch square baking pan. SPOON 1 tablespoon cheese filling into the center of each crepe. FOLD each crepe into a 6-inch roll. PLACE seam side down in the prepared pan. POUR 1 cup of the remaining tomato sauce over the crepes. SPRINKLE with mozzarella cheese. BAKE at 350 degrees for 25 to 30 minutes or until heated through. HEAT the remaining tomato sauce in a saucepan. SERVE with the manicotti.

Rigatoni in a Woodsman's Sauce

YIELD: 6 SERVINGS

4 ounces sweet or hot Italian sausage
3 tablespoons olive oil
$^{1}/_{2}$ cup chopped onion
2 cups sliced assorted mushrooms
2 tablespoons unsalted butter
1 (28-ounce) can Italian tomatoes, crushed
$^{1}/_{2}$ cup ricotta cheese
1 cup half-and-half
1 (10-ounce) package frozen peas, thawed
Salt and freshly ground pepper to taste
1 pound rigatoni
1 cup freshly grated Parmigiano-Reggiano

REMOVE the casings from the sausage and discard. CRUMBLE the sausage. HEAT the olive oil in a large stockpot. ADD the onion. SAUTÉ over medium heat until wilted. ADD the sausage. COOK for 10 minutes; drain. ADD the mushrooms and butter. COOK for 3 minutes. ADD the tomatoes. REDUCE the heat to low. SIMMER for 10 minutes or until thickened, stirring constantly. STIR in $^{1}/_{4}$ cup of the ricotta cheese. ADD the half-and-half and peas. SIMMER for 4 to 5 minutes. SEASON with salt and pepper to taste. COOK the rigatoni using the package directions until al dente. DRAIN the pasta and place in a large serving bowl. POUR the sauce over the pasta and toss to mix well. FOLD in the Parmigiano-Reggiano and the remaining $^{1}/_{4}$ cup ricotta cheese. SERVE immediately.

Chicken, Ham and Asparagus Lasagna

YIELD: 6 TO 8 SERVINGS

1/3 cup butter
1 cup sliced mushrooms
1/2 cup flour
2 tablespoons minced onion
2 garlic cloves, minced
2 cups chicken broth
1 cup milk
1/2 cup grated Parmesan cheese
Salt and pepper to taste
12 lasagna noodles, cooked, drained
3 cups shredded cooked chicken (2 whole chicken breasts)
8 ounces thinly sliced cooked ham
2 (10-ounce) packages frozen cut asparagus, thawed, drained
8 ounces sliced mozzarella cheese
1/2 cup grated Parmesan cheese

MELT the butter in a large saucepan. ADD the mushrooms. SAUTÉ for 3 to 4 minutes. WHISK in the flour, onion and garlic. SAUTÉ for 2 to 3 minutes. ADD the broth and milk 1 cup at a time, stirring constantly. COOK until thickened, stirring constantly. ADD 1/2 cup Parmesan cheese. SEASON with salt and pepper to taste. SPOON 3/4 cup of the sauce in a lightly greased 9x13-inch baking pan. RESERVE 3 lasagna noodles and 3/4 cup of the sauce. LAYER the remaining noodles, chicken, ham, asparagus, mozzarella cheese and remaining sauce 1/3 at a time in the prepared pan. ARRANGE the reserved noodles over the layers. SPREAD with the reserved sauce. SPRINKLE with 1/2 cup Parmesan cheese. BAKE at 350 degrees for 30 to 35 minutes or until heated through. LET stand for 10 to 15 minutes before serving.

Pasta and Grilled Chicken Caesar

YIELD: 12 SERVINGS

1 (6-ounce) jar marinated artichoke
   hearts
½ cup olive oil
¼ cup vegetable oil
¼ cup lemon juice
1 teaspoon salt
½ teaspoon pepper
¼ teaspoon sugar

10 ounces vermicelli, cooked, drained
2 garlic cloves, minced
1 small bunch romaine lettuce, cut
   into narrow slices crosswise
4 chicken breast halves, grilled, sliced
½ cup grated Parmesan cheese
1 cup Caesar croutons

DRAIN the artichoke hearts, reserving the marinade. CHOP the artichoke hearts. COMBINE the reserved marinade, olive oil, vegetable oil, lemon juice, salt, pepper and sugar in a bowl and mix well. STIR in the artichoke hearts. COMBINE the pasta, garlic, romaine, chicken and Parmesan cheese in a large bowl and toss to mix well. ADD the artichoke mixture and toss to mix well. CHILL until serving time. SPRINKLE with the croutons just before serving.

Pasta with Tuna Sauce

YIELD: 2 TO 4 SERVINGS

1 bunch green onions, finely chopped
¼ cup olive oil
1 cup canned tomatoes
1 (3-ounce) can olive oil-pack tuna,
   drained, flaked

¼ teaspoon dried basil
8 to 12 ounces angel hair pasta,
   cooked, drained

SAUTÉ the green onions in the olive oil in a skillet until tender. ADD the tomatoes. SIMMER for 10 minutes. ADD the tuna and basil. SIMMER for 10 minutes, stirring frequently. SPOON over the hot pasta and toss to mix well. SERVE immediately.

Tortellini with Smoked Salmon and Dill

YIELD: 2 TO 4 SERVINGS

¹/₄ cup butter
2 shallots, minced
4 ounces smoked salmon, cut into thin strips
1 small bunch fresh dill, chopped

1 cup heavy cream
1 pound cheese tortellini, cooked, drained
¹/₈ teaspoon grated fresh nutmeg
1 sprig of fresh dill

MELT the butter in a medium saucepan. ADD the shallots. SAUTÉ for 2 to 3 minutes or until softened. REDUCE the heat to medium-low. STIR in the salmon, chopped dill and cream. HEAT for a few minutes, being careful not to scald the cream. FOLD into the hot tortellini in a large bowl. SPRINKLE with nutmeg. GARNISH with a sprig of dill.

Salmon Tetrazzini

YIELD: 6 SERVINGS

¹/₃ cup chopped onion
3 tablespoons olive oil or vegetable oil
¹/₄ cup flour
1¹/₄ teaspoons seasoned salt
¹/₈ teaspoon thyme
Pepper to taste
2 cups half-and-half
1¹/₂ tablespoons sherry

2 (6-ounce) cans pink salmon, drained, flaked
¹/₂ cup sliced black olives
¹/₄ cup chopped green bell pepper
4 ounces spaghetti, cooked, drained
¹/₃ cup grated Parmesan cheese
Paprika to taste
Chopped fresh parsley to taste

SAUTÉ the onion in the olive oil for 5 minutes. STIR in the flour, seasoned salt, thyme and pepper. COOK over low heat until smooth and bubbly, stirring constantly. REMOVE from the heat. STIR in the half-and-half. COOK over low heat until thickened and smooth, stirring constantly. STIR in the sherry, salmon, black olives and green pepper. ADD the hot spaghetti and toss to mix well. SPOON into a buttered 1¹/₂-quart baking dish. SPRINKLE with Parmesan cheese and paprika. BAKE at 350 degrees for 20 to 25 minutes or until heated through. GARNISH with chopped parsley.

Spaghetti with Scallops, Roasted Red Peppers and Pine Nuts

YIELD: 2 SERVINGS

2 red bell peppers
3 tablespoons virgin olive oil
$1/2$ cup olive oil
12 ounces sea or bay scallops
2 teaspoons lemon juice
Salt and freshly ground pepper to taste
6 to 8 ounces spaghetti or linguini, cooked, drained
$1/2$ cup pine nuts, toasted
2 teaspoons chopped fresh chives, or
2 tablespoons chopped fresh parsley

CHAR the red peppers over an open flame until blackened on all sides. PLACE in a nonrecyled paper bag and close the bag. LET the peppers steam for 15 to 20 minutes. PEEL the skins from the red peppers. CUT the red peppers into halves. REMOVE the stems and discard the seeds. CUT the red peppers into $1/4$x3-inch strips and place in a bowl. ADD 3 tablespoons virgin olive oil. MARINATE, covered, for several minutes to 12 hours. HEAT $1/2$ cup olive oil in a large skillet over high heat. ADD the scallops. SEAR for about 1 minute on each side. ADD the roasted red peppers with some of the marinade and the lemon juice. COOK until heated through. SEASON with salt and pepper. POUR the sauce over the hot pasta in a serving bowl. ADD the pine nuts and toss to mix well. SPRINKLE with the chives. SERVE immediately.

Shrimp Fettuccini

YIELD: 4 TO 6 SERVINGS

1 garlic clove, minced
1 tablespoon olive oil
1 yellow or red bell pepper, chopped
1 medium onion, chopped
1 pound shrimp, peeled, deveined

2 (15-ounce) cans diced Italian tomatoes
12 ounces fettuccini, cooked
Parmesan cheese to taste

SAUTÉ the garlic in the olive oil in a skillet. ADD the yellow pepper and onion. SAUTÉ for 5 minutes. ADD the shrimp. SAUTÉ for 5 minutes or until the shrimp turn pink. ADD the tomatoes. COOK until heated through and some of the liquid has evaporated. SPOON over the hot fettuccini in a serving bowl and toss to mix well. SPRINKLE with Parmesan cheese. SERVE immediately.

Shrimp and Artichoke Primavera

YIELD: 6 SERVINGS

3 tablespoons olive oil
1 cup chopped carrots
1 cup chopped celery
1 cup chopped onion
3 garlic cloves, minced
$3^{1}/_{2}$ cups canned crushed Italian tomatoes
$^{1}/_{2}$ teaspoon salt

$^{1}/_{4}$ teaspoon pepper
8 ounces medium shrimp, peeled, deveined
1 cup drained canned sliced artichoke hearts
Chopped fresh basil to taste
1 pound linguini, cooked, drained
Freshly grated Romano cheese to taste

HEAT 2 tablespoons of the olive oil in a large skillet over high heat. ADD the carrots, celery, onion and garlic. SAUTÉ for 4 to 5 minutes or until the carrots are tender-crisp. ADD the tomatoes, salt and pepper. BRING to a boil. ADD the shrimp and artichokes. COOK for 2 to 3 minutes or until the shrimp turn pink. REDUCE the heat to low. SIMMER for 2 minutes. SPRINKLE with basil. TOSS the hot linguini with the remaining 1 tablespoon olive oil in a large serving bowl. ADD the shrimp sauce and toss to mix well. SPRINKLE with Romano cheese.

Greek-Style Shrimp with Pasta

YIELD: 4 SERVINGS

1 teaspoon finely chopped garlic
5 tablespoons olive oil
2 cups cubed peeled tomatoes
1/2 cup dry white wine
Salt and black pepper to taste
3/4 cup finely chopped fresh basil

1 teaspoon dried crumbled oregano
1 1/2 pounds medium shrimp, peeled, deveined
1/8 teaspoon hot red pepper flakes
8 ounces crumbled feta cheese
6 ounces rigatoni, cooked, drained

SAUTÉ the garlic in 2 tablespoons of the olive oil in a skillet. ADD the tomatoes. COOK for 1 minute. ADD the wine, salt, pepper, basil and oregano. COOK over medium heat for 10 minutes. SEASON the shrimp with salt and pepper. HEAT the remaining 3 tablespoons olive oil in a large skillet. ADD the shrimp. SAUTÉ for 1 minute or until the shrimp turn pink. SPRINKLE with red pepper flakes. SPOON into a small baking dish. SPRINKLE with feta cheese. SPOON the tomato sauce over the top. BAKE at 400 degrees for 10 minutes or until bubbly. SPOON over the hot pasta on a serving platter.

Pasta with Shrimp and Feta

YIELD: 4 SERVINGS

1 pound shrimp, peeled, deveined
1 pound penne
1 (10-ounce) package frozen peas
1 cup crumbled feta cheese
1/2 cup sliced black olives

1 red bell pepper, julienned
2 to 3 tablespoons olive oil
Chopped fresh basil (optional)
Freshly grated Parmesan cheese
Freshly ground pepper to taste

COOK the shrimp in boiling water in a saucepan until the shrimp turn pink; drain. COOK the pasta in boiling water in a saucepan for 7 minutes. ADD the peas. COOK for 2 to 3 minutes longer or until the pasta is al dente; drain and return to the saucepan. ADD the feta cheese, black olives, red pepper and shrimp. STIR until the feta cheese begins to become creamy, adding enough olive oil to prevent the pasta from sticking. SPOON into a large serving bowl. SPRINKLE with basil, Parmesan cheese and pepper.

Seafood Lasagna

YIELD: 6 TO 8 SERVINGS

1 large onion, chopped
2 tablespoons butter
8 ounces cream cheese, softened
1 1/2 cups ricotta cheese
1 egg, beaten
2 teaspoons dried basil
1/2 teaspoon salt
1/8 teaspoon pepper
2 (10-ounce) cans cream of mushroom soup
1/3 cup milk
1/3 cup dry white wine
8 ounces frozen crabmeat
8 ounces shrimp, peeled, deveined
8 ounces scallops
1/4 cup grated or shredded Parmesan cheese
8 lasagna noodles, cooked, drained
1/2 cup shredded mozzarella cheese

SAUTÉ the onion in the butter in a skillet until tender and place in a bowl. ADD the cream cheese, ricotta cheese, egg, basil, salt and pepper and mix well. COMBINE the soup, milk and wine in a bowl and mix well. STIR in the crabmeat, shrimp, scallops and Parmesan cheese. LAYER the noodles, cream cheese mixture and seafood mixture 1/2 at a time in a 9x13-inch baking dish. SPRINKLE with mozzarella cheese. BAKE at 325 degrees for 1 1/4 hours. LET stand for 10 to 15 minutes before serving.

NOTE: Can assemble the day before serving and store, covered, in the refrigerator. BAKE just before serving.

Layered Pasta Ricotta Pie

YIELD: 6 TO 8 SERVINGS

4 ounces vermicelli
1 tablespoon olive or vegetable oil
1/3 cup finely chopped green onions
4 garlic cloves, minced
1/2 cup grated Parmesan cheese or Romano cheese
1 egg, beaten
1 (10-ounce) package frozen chopped spinach, thawed
2 egg yolks
15 ounces ricotta cheese
1/2 teaspoon salt
1/2 cup grated Parmesan cheese
2 egg whites, stiffly beaten
1 1/2 cups spaghetti sauce

BREAK the vermicelli into thirds. COOK using package directions until al dente; drain. HEAT the olive oil in a large skillet over medium heat. ADD the green onions and garlic. SAUTÉ until tender. REMOVE from the heat. ADD the hot vermicelli, 1/2 cup Parmesan cheese and 1 egg and toss to mix well. PRESS over the bottom of a well greased 9-inch springform pan. DRAIN the spinach well and pat dry. COMBINE 2 egg yolks, ricotta cheese, spinach, salt and 1/2 cup Parmesan cheese in a bowl and mix well. SPREAD over the pasta layer. BEAT 2 egg whites in a small mixer bowl until stiff peaks form. FOLD into the spaghetti sauce in a bowl. POUR over the spinach mixture. BAKE at 350 degrees for 50 to 60 minutes or until set. LET stand for 10 minutes. REMOVE the side of the pan. SERVE with additional heated spaghetti sauce if desired.

Pasta with Broccoli and Goat Cheese

YIELD: 4 TO 6 SERVINGS

6 cups packed broccoli florets
3/4 cup unsalted butter, cut into pieces
1 pound creamy goat cheese, cut into pieces

1 pound fettuccini or medium to large pasta shells, cooked, drained
Salt and freshly ground pepper to taste

PARBOIL the broccoli in water in a saucepan for 30 seconds or until tender-crisp; drain. MELT the butter in a large skillet over medium heat. ADD the broccoli and toss until coated with the butter. COOK for 2 minutes or until heated through. ADD the goat cheese. COOK until the goat cheese melts, stirring constantly to coat the broccoli. POUR over the hot pasta in a large serving bowl. SEASON with salt and pepper to taste.

Mushroom Saffron Sauce over Fettuccini

YIELD: 2 SERVINGS

1 tablespoon unsalted butter
1/4 cup minced shallots
8 ounces sliced assorted mushrooms
1 cup chicken broth
1/2 teaspoon saffron threads
1/4 teaspoon thyme

1/8 teaspoon ground allspice
1/2 cup heavy cream
Salt and pepper to taste
6 to 8 ounces spinach fettuccini, cooked, drained
1/4 cup shredded asiago cheese

MELT the butter in a large skillet. ADD the shallots and mushrooms. SAUTÉ over high heat for 1 to 2 minutes or until brown. ADD 1/2 cup of the chicken broth. COVER the skillet and reduce the heat to low. SIMMER for 5 minutes or until the mushrooms are tender. HEAT the remaining 1/2 cup chicken broth in a saucepan until hot. ADD the saffron. HEAT until the saffron is dissolved. ADD to the skillet with the thyme, allspice, cream, salt and pepper. SIMMER until slightly thickened, stirring constantly. PLACE the pasta in 2 individual serving bowls. SPOON the sauce over each serving and sprinkle with asiago cheese. SERVE immediately.

Linguini with Tomato and Basil Sauce

YIELD: 4 TO 6 SERVINGS

1 medium onion, chopped
1 to 2 garlic cloves, crushed
2 tablespoons vegetable oil
1 (28-ounce) can whole tomatoes, cut into quarters
2 tablespoons chopped sweet basil
1 tablespoon sugar
1 cup heavy cream
1/4 cup butter
12 to 16 ounces linguini, cooked, drained
Grated Parmesan cheese (optional)

SAUTÉ the onion and garlic in the vegetable oil in a skillet until the onion is translucent. ADD the tomatoes, basil and sugar. COOK for 10 minutes. ADD the cream and butter. COOK for 10 minutes or until heated through, stirring constantly. POUR over the hot linguini in a large serving bowl and toss to coat well. SPRINKLE with Parmesan cheese.

Linguini with Sun-Dried Tomato Pesto

YIELD: 4 SERVINGS

1 cup drained oil-pack sun-dried tomatoes
1/2 cup grated Romano cheese or Parmesan cheese
1/4 cup chopped fresh basil, or 1 tablespoon dried basil
2 tablespoons pine nuts, toasted
3 garlic cloves
3/4 cup olive oil
12 ounces linguini
Salt and pepper to taste

COMBINE the sun-dried tomatoes, Romano cheese, basil, pine nuts and garlic in a food processor container. ADD the olive oil gradually, processing constantly to form a smooth paste. MAY cover and store in the refrigerator for up to 2 weeks. COOK the linguini in salted boiling water in a saucepan until al dente. DRAIN, reserving 1/2 cup of the liquid. COMBINE 3/4 cup of the tomato pesto and the reserved liquid in the saucepan. ADD the drained linguini and toss over medium heat to coat, adding additional tomato pesto if desired. SEASON with salt and pepper.

Pasta with Spicy Tomato Cream Sauce

YIELD: 6 TO 8 SERVINGS

4 garlic cloves, minced
1/2 teaspoon red pepper
1/4 cup olive oil
1 (28-ounce) can crushed tomatoes

1 pound pasta, cooked, drained
2 tablespoons vodka
1 cup heavy cream
1/4 cup chopped fresh parsley

SAUTÉ the garlic and red pepper in the olive oil in a skillet until the garlic is golden brown. ADD the tomatoes. SIMMER until thickened, stirring constantly. ADD the pasta and toss to coat well. ADD the vodka and cream gradually, tossing to coat well after each addition. COVER and reduce the heat. COOK for 2 to 3 minutes. ADD the parsley and toss well. SERVE immediately.

Marinara Sauce

YIELD: 6 TO 8 SERVINGS

2 large shallots, chopped
2 tablespoons olive oil
2 (28-ounce) cans chopped Italian
    tomatoes
1/2 cup chopped fresh basil, or
    1 1/2 tablespoons dried basil
2 bay leaves
2 tablespoons tomato paste

2 tablespoons sugar
3 tablespoons chopped fresh oregano,
    or 1 tablespoon dried oregano
2 tablespoons chopped fresh
    marjoram, or 2 teaspoons dried
    marjoram
1 teaspoon salt

SAUTÉ the shallots in the olive oil in a skillet. ADD the tomatoes, basil, bay leaves, tomato paste, sugar, oregano, marjoram and salt. SIMMER for 20 minutes, stirring occasionally. REMOVE and discard the bay leaves. SERVE over your favorite cooked pasta.

Side Dishes

THE GAME PLAN

MENU

SKYLINE® CHILI DIP – *PAGE 30*

ROMAINE SALAD WITH SWEET AND TANGY MUSTARD DRESSING – *PAGE 52*

SPICY SESAME TERIYAKI SHISH KABOBS – *PAGE 66*

BLEU CHEESE AND BACON POTATOES – *PAGE 111*

CHILI PECAN BISCUITS – *PAGE 127*

BANANA CAKE WITH CARAMEL FROSTING – *PAGE 144*

CHOCOLATE CRANBERRY COOKIES – *PAGE 158*

OHIO STATE UNIVERSITY

Home of Ohio State Buckeye football since 1922, the giant horseshoe-shaped Ohio Stadium is one of college football's most recognizable landmarks. The exciting rituals of the "Buckeye Battle Cry," dotting the "i" in the famous "Script Ohio" marching band formation, the ringing of the Ohio State University Victory Bell, and the cheering of nearly 100,000 fans fill the fabled Ohio Stadium. "Affirm Thy Friendship, O.H.I.O!" GO BUCKS!

Broccoli Mops with Ginger Sauce

YIELD: 4 SERVINGS

Salt to taste
1 large bunch broccoli, cut into florets
2 teaspoons cornstarch
1 cup canned beef broth
1 tablespoon dry sherry
1 tablespoon soy sauce
2 teaspoons rice vinegar
1 teaspoon sugar
1 tablespoon minced fresh ginger
1 medium garlic clove, minced
1 teaspoon vegetable oil
1 teaspoon sesame oil
3 medium green onions, thinly sliced

BRING lightly salted water to a boil in a large saucepan over high heat. ADD the broccoli. RETURN to a boil. COOK for 3 minutes or until tender. REMOVE from the heat and cover with foil to keep warm. MIX the cornstarch, beef broth, sherry, soy sauce, vinegar and sugar in a small bowl. SAUTÉ the ginger and garlic in the vegetable oil in a small saucepan over medium heat for 1 minute. STIR in the cornstarch mixture. BRING to a boil. COOK over medium heat until thickened, stirring constantly. STIR in the sesame oil and green onions. REMOVE from the heat. DRAIN the warm broccoli. ADD the sauce and toss until the broccoli is coated well. SPOON into a serving dish. SERVE immediately.

Orange-Glazed Carrots

YIELD: 6 TO 8 SERVINGS

2 (1-pound) packages baby carrots
2/3 cup sugar
2 tablespoons flour
Grated peel of 1 orange

1½ cups orange juice
¼ cup butter, cut into small pieces
Salt and freshly ground pepper
    to taste

STEAM the carrots in a steamer over boiling water until tender. DRAIN and keep hot in a serving bowl. COMBINE the sugar, flour and orange peel in a small saucepan. WHISK in the orange juice. BRING to a simmer over medium-high heat. SIMMER until thickened, stirring constantly. WHISK in the butter. POUR over the hot carrots. SEASON with salt and pepper. SERVE immediately.

Horseradish Carrots

YIELD: 8 SERVINGS

14 to 16 carrots, cut diagonally into
    1-inch slices, or 2 pounds baby
    carrots
2 tablespoons finely chopped onion
1 tablespoon prepared horseradish, or
    to taste

2/3 cup mayonnaise
2 cups herbed stuffing crumbs
Salt and freshly ground pepper
    to taste
¼ cup butter, cut into small pieces

COOK the carrots in water to cover in a saucepan until tender. DRAIN, reserving ½ cup of the liquid. PLACE the carrots in an ovenproof baking dish sprayed with butter-flavor cooking spray. COMBINE the onion, horseradish and mayonnaise in a bowl and mix well. POUR over the carrots. SPRINKLE the stuffing crumbs, salt and pepper over the sauce. SPRINKLE with the reserved liquid. DOT with the butter. BAKE at 350 degrees for 20 to 25 minutes or until bubbly.

Corn Pudding

YIELD: 6 SERVINGS

3 tablespoons butter, softened
2 tablespoons sugar
2 tablespoons flour
1 teaspoon salt

3 eggs
2 cups frozen white Shoe Peg corn
3/4 cup milk

COMBINE the butter, sugar, flour and salt in a bowl and mix well. ADD the eggs and mix well. STIR in the corn and milk. POUR into a buttered baking dish. BAKE at 350 degrees for 45 minutes or until the top is golden brown and a knife inserted in the center comes out clean, stirring once halfway through the baking time.

NOTE: Can prepare the pudding the night before and store, covered, in the refrigerator until ready to bake.

Barbecued Green Beans

YIELD: 12 SERVINGS

6 slices lean bacon, cut into pieces
1 medium onion, chopped
1/2 cup packed brown sugar

1/2 cup catsup
4 (16-ounce) cans cut green beans

SAUTÉ the bacon in a skillet until crisp. ADD the onion. SAUTÉ until the onion is tender; drain. STIR in the brown sugar and catsup. COMBINE with the green beans in a large bowl and mix well. SPOON into a 2-quart baking dish. BAKE, covered, at 250 degrees for 2 hours. DO not overbake. SERVE immediately.

Green Beans Provençal

YIELD: 4 SERVINGS

1¹/₂ pounds green beans
¹/₂ teaspoon salt
2 tablespoons olive oil
¹/₂ teaspoon minced garlic

¹/₂ teaspoon crumbled dried thyme
Juice of ¹/₂ lemon
¹/₂ lemon, thinly sliced (optional)

TRIM the green beans and cut into halves. BRING a large saucepan of water to a boil. ADD the salt and green beans. COOK for 4 to 5 minutes or until the green beans are tender-crisp and bright green. DO not overcook. POUR the green beans into a colander and rinse immediately under cold running water. HEAT the olive oil in a large skillet. ADD the garlic, thyme and lemon juice. ADD the green beans and toss to mix well. SAUTÉ for 1 to 1¹/₂ minutes or until the green beans are heated through. DO not overcook. SPOON into a serving dish and garnish with lemon slices. SERVE immediately.

NOTE: Can add ¹/₂ red bell pepper, diced, when sautéing.

Good-For-You Refried Beans

YIELD: 10 TO 12 SERVINGS

1 tablespoon canola oil
1 large onion, chopped
¹/₂ green or red bell pepper, chopped
2 ribs celery, chopped
2 carrots, chopped

1 (48-ounce) can pinto beans,
    mashed
Soy sauce to taste
2 tablespoons chopped fresh parsley
¹/₃ cup salsa (optional)

HEAT the canola oil in a large skillet over medium-low heat. ADD the onion, green pepper, celery and carrots. COOK until the vegetables are soft. STIR in the mashed beans. SEASON with soy sauce. SIMMER, covered, for 5 minutes. INCREASE the heat to medium-high. BRING to a boil, stirring constantly. COOK until the mixture is of a creamy consistency and the liquid is reduced, stirring constantly. REMOVE from the heat. STIR in the parsley and salsa.

Mushrooms in Wine Sauce

YIELD: 4 SERVINGS

1 tablespoon butter
1 pound mushrooms
2 tablespoons sauterne or white wine

1/2 teaspoon salt
1 to 2 grinds of black peppercorns

MELT the butter in a skillet over high heat. ADD the mushrooms. SAUTÉ for 2 to 3 minutes. ADD the wine, salt and pepper. COOK for 10 minutes or until the mushrooms are tender. SERVE immediately.

Sautéed Peas with Walnuts

YIELD: 4 TO 6 SERVINGS

1 tablespoon unsalted butter
1 large shallot, minced
1/4 cup chicken stock or broth
2 teaspoons honey
1 (10-ounce) package frozen petite point or baby peas

2 or 3 drops of Tabasco sauce
Salt and freshly ground pepper to taste
1/2 cup chopped toasted walnuts

MELT the butter in a skillet over medium-low heat. ADD the shallot. SAUTÉ for 3 minutes. ADD the chicken stock and honey. INCREASE the heat to medium-high. STIR in the peas. SAUTÉ until the peas are tender and the liquid evaporates. SEASON with Tabasco sauce, salt and pepper. REMOVE from the heat. FOLD in the walnuts. SERVE immediately.

Bleu Cheese and Bacon Potatoes

YIELD: 8 SERVINGS

4 medium potatoes
2 to 3 tablespoons butter, softened
1/2 cup sour cream
1/4 cup crumbled bleu cheese
1/4 cup milk

1/4 cup butter, softened
1/4 teaspoon salt
1/4 teaspoon freshly ground pepper
4 slices bacon, crisp-cooked, crumbled

SCRUB the potatoes and pat dry. RUB with 2 to 3 tablespoons butter. BAKE at 400 degrees for 1 hour or until tender. CUT the potatoes into halves lengthwise. SCOOP out the pulp, leaving a 1/4-inch shell. RESERVE the shells. MASH the potato pulp in a mixer bowl. ADD the sour cream, bleu cheese, milk, 1/4 cup butter, salt and pepper. BEAT until fluffy. SPOON into the reserved potato shells. PLACE on a lightly greased baking sheet. BAKE for 15 minutes. SPRINKLE with the bacon. SERVE immediately.

Potato and Carrot Pudding

YIELD: 4 TO 6 SERVINGS

8 carrots, sliced (1 1/4 pounds)
2 potatoes, peeled, sliced (1 1/2 pounds)
1 egg, lightly beaten
2 tablespoons grated onion
2 tablespoons sour cream

1/2 to 3/4 teaspoon salt
1/4 teaspoon freshly ground pepper
1/2 cup shredded Cheddar cheese
1 tablespoon butter, chopped
Carrot curls
Sprigs of fresh parsley

BRING the carrots to a boil in water to cover in a large saucepan. COOK, covered, for 10 minutes. ADD the potatoes. COOK, covered, for 10 minutes or until the vegetables are tender; drain. MASH the vegetables. COMBINE the egg, onion, sour cream, salt and pepper in a large bowl and mix well. ADD the mashed vegetables. FOLD in the Cheddar cheese. SPOON into a lightly greased 1 1/2-quart baking dish. BAKE at 350 degrees for 30 minutes. DOT with butter. BROIL for 10 minutes. GARNISH with carrot curls and parsley.

Mashed Red Potatoes

YIELD: 4 TO 6 SERVINGS

1 1/2 pounds small red potatoes
1/2 teaspoon salt
1/2 cup half-and-half
1 tablespoon unsalted butter

Salt and freshly ground pepper
  to taste
1 tablespoon chopped fresh parsley

SCRUB the potatoes and pat dry. CUT the unpeeled potatoes into quarters and place in a saucepan. ADD enough water to cover and sprinkle with 1/2 teaspoon salt. BRING to a boil and reduce the heat. SIMMER for 12 to 18 minutes or until tender. DRAIN the potatoes and return to the saucepan. HEAT the half-and-half and butter in a small saucepan until the butter melts, stirring constantly. POUR over the potatoes. MASH the potatoes to a chunky consistency. SEASON with salt and pepper to taste. SPRINKLE with parsley.

Roasted Red Bell Peppers

YIELD: 4 SERVINGS

4 firm red bell peppers
1/2 cup olive oil

2 garlic cloves, finely minced
1 tablespoon minced fresh parsley

RINSE the red peppers and pat dry. PLACE on a baking sheet. BROIL until the sides of the red peppers are charred. REMOVE from the oven. LET stand until cool. REMOVE the charred skin from the red peppers. DISCARD the stems and seeds. RINSE the red peppers under cool water and pat dry. CUT the red peppers into 1/2-inch strips. COMBINE the olive oil, garlic and parsley in a bowl and mix well. ADD the red pepper strips and toss to coat well. SERVE at room temperature.

Spinach Delight

YIELD: 8 TO 10 SERVINGS

3 (10-ounce) packages frozen spinach
1/2 cup chopped onion
1/4 cup butter
3/4 cup soft bread crumbs
1 cup half-and-half

1/2 cup coarsely chopped pecans
1 teaspoon salt
1/2 teaspoon ground nutmeg
1/8 teaspoon pepper
2 teaspoons melted butter

THAW the spinach and squeeze out any excess moisture. SAUTÉ the onion in 1/4 cup butter in a skillet until translucent. COMBINE with the spinach, 1/2 cup of the bread crumbs, half-and-half, pecans, salt, nutmeg and pepper in a large bowl and mix well. SPOON into a buttered 1 1/2-quart shallow baking dish. TOP with a mixture of the remaining bread crumbs and 2 teaspoons butter. BAKE at 350 degrees for 30 minutes.

Tomato Pie

YIELD: 6 SERVINGS

1 recipe (1-crust) pie pastry
4 medium tomatoes, sliced, drained
1 1/2 teaspoons basil
1 teaspoon oregano
1/4 teaspoon salt

1/4 teaspoon pepper
1 cup shredded mozzarella cheese
1/4 cup chopped scallions
1/2 cup mayonnaise

LINE a pie plate with the pastry. TRIM and flute the edge. BAKE at 425 degrees for 5 minutes. REMOVE from the oven. REDUCE the oven temperature to 400 degrees. LAYER the drained tomatoes in the partially baked pie pastry. SPRINKLE with basil, oregano, salt and pepper. COMBINE the mozzarella cheese, scallions and mayonnaise in a bowl and mix well. SPREAD evenly over the tomatoes, sealing to the edge. BAKE for 35 minutes. LET stand for 10 minutes before serving.

NOTE: Can use light or reduced-fat mayonnaise.

Roasted Rosemary Vegetables

YIELD: 6 TO 8 SERVINGS

12 small red potatoes
2 sweet potatoes
4 carrots
4 parsnips
4 beets

4 small turnips
Olive oil
1 to 2 teaspoons salt
Freshly ground pepper to taste
Sprigs of fresh rosemary

SCRUB the red potatoes. CUT the red potatoes into halves. PEEL the remaining vegetables and pat dry. CUT into pieces about the same size as the red potatoes. COMBINE all the vegetables in a large bowl with enough olive oil to lightly coat. SEASON with salt and pepper. SPRINKLE with rosemary. PLACE in a single layer on a large baking sheet. BAKE at 375 degrees for 40 to 45 minutes or until the vegetables are tender when pierced with a fork.

Southern Yam Bake

YIELD: 4 TO 6 SERVINGS

½ cup packed brown sugar
½ cup flour
½ teaspoon grated nutmeg
2 tablespoons butter
½ cup chopped toasted pecans

2 (17-ounce) cans yams, drained
1 (16-ounce) can sliced peaches, drained
1½ cups miniature marshmallows

COMBINE the brown sugar, flour and nutmeg in a bowl. CUT in the butter until crumbly. STIR in the toasted pecans. ARRANGE the yams and peaches in a buttered 1½-quart baking dish. SPRINKLE with the brown sugar mixture. BAKE at 350 degrees for 35 minutes. SPRINKLE the marshmallows over the top. BROIL until the marshmallows are light brown, watching carefully.

Sun-Dried Tomato Polenta Gratin

YIELD: 6 SERVINGS

Salt to taste
7$\frac{1}{2}$ cups water
2$\frac{1}{4}$ cups yellow cornmeal
6 tablespoons unsalted butter
6 tablespoons freshly grated
  Parmesan cheese
$\frac{1}{4}$ cup coarsely chopped sun-dried
  tomatoes
1 to 2 tablespoons finely chopped
  fresh basil
Pepper to taste

BRING lightly salted water to a boil in a saucepan. SPRINKLE in the cornmeal gradually, stirring constantly to prevent lumping. REDUCE the heat. SIMMER for 15 minutes, stirring constantly. REMOVE from the heat. STIR in $\frac{1}{2}$ of the butter, $\frac{1}{2}$ of the Parmesan cheese, tomatoes and basil. SEASON with salt and pepper to taste. POUR into a 2-quart shallow baking dish. DOT with the remaining butter. SPRINKLE with the remaining Parmesan cheese. BAKE at 350 degrees for 10 to 15 minutes or until set.

NOTE: Can reduce the recipe by half or double the recipe.

Rice Delmonico

YIELD: 6 SERVINGS

4 cups cooked rice
1 cup chopped green onions
6 slices bacon, crisp-cooked, crumbled
$\frac{1}{3}$ cup chopped pimentos or red bell
  pepper
1 cup sour cream
1 tablespoon melted butter
1 teaspoon basil
$\frac{1}{2}$ teaspoon salt
$\frac{1}{4}$ teaspoon pepper

COMBINE the rice, green onions, bacon, pimentos, sour cream, butter, basil, salt and pepper in a bowl and mix well. SPOON into a buttered 2-quart baking dish. BAKE, covered, at 400 degrees for 20 minutes or until heated through.

NOTE: Can prepare and chill, covered, until baking time. Bring to room temperature before baking.

Garlic Rice

YIELD: 4 SERVINGS

2 garlic cloves, minced
2 tablespoons olive oil
1 cup long grain rice

2 cups chicken broth
Salt and pepper to taste
Minced fresh parsley to taste

SAUTÉ the garlic in the olive oil in a medium saucepan over medium heat until softened. STIR in the rice. ADD the chicken broth. BRING to a boil. COVER and reduce the heat to low. COOK for 17 to 20 minutes or until the rice is tender and the broth is absorbed. STIR in the salt, pepper and parsley.

Lemon Rice

YIELD: 4 SERVINGS

1/4 cup finely chopped onion
1 medium carrot, finely chopped
1 rib celery, finely chopped
2 cups chicken broth or water

1 cup long grain rice
Juice of 1 lemon (about 3 tablespoons)
1/4 teaspoon salt
1 bay leaf

SAUTÉ the onion, carrot and celery in a large skillet sprayed with nonstick cooking spray for 2 minutes. ADD the chicken broth, rice, lemon juice, salt and bay leaf. BRING to a boil and reduce the heat. SIMMER, covered, for 20 minutes or until the rice is tender and the liquid is absorbed. REMOVE and discard the bay leaf before serving.

Rice with Mushrooms and Onions

YIELD: 6 SERVINGS

2 cups white rice
1 (10-ounce) can beef broth
1 (10-ounce) can French onion soup
½ cup butter or margarine

1 cup sliced fresh mushrooms, or
  1 (6-ounce) can sliced button
  mushrooms, drained

COMBINE the rice, beef broth, French onion soup, butter and mushrooms in a microwave-safe dish. MICROWAVE on High for 25 minutes.

NOTE: Can bake at 350 degrees for 45 to 60 minutes or until liquid is absorbed.

Microwave Risotto

YIELD: 4 SERVINGS

1 small onion, chopped
1 garlic clove, minced (optional)
3 tablespoons olive oil

1 cup arborio rice
2 cups chicken broth
¼ cup grated Parmesan cheese

COMBINE the onion, garlic and olive oil in a glass dish. MICROWAVE, covered, on High for 1 to 2 minutes or until the onion is tender. STIR in the rice. ADD the broth. MICROWAVE, covered, on High until the broth begins to boil. MICROWAVE on Medium until most of the liquid is absorbed. STIR in the Parmesan cheese. LET stand for 5 minutes before serving.

NOTE: Can add vegetables (such as frozen peas, sliced mushrooms, sliced or shredded carrots or asparagus), cooked chicken, cooked sausage and seafood to risotto to serve as a main dish.

Honey Mustard

YIELD: 6 TO 8 OUNCES

3/4 cup Dijon mustard
1/4 cup vegetable oil

1/4 cup honey
2 tablespoons dry mustard

COMBINE the Dijon mustard, vegetable oil, honey and dry mustard in a 1-quart saucepan. BRING just to a boil, stirring constantly. REMOVE from the heat. LET stand until cool. SPOON into hot sterilized jars, leaving 1/2 inch headspace; seal with 2-piece lids. STORE in the refrigerator.

NOTE: Serve with meats. Can also thin with cream and serve as a sauce.

Peach Catsup

YIELD: 1 CUP

1 (16-ounce) can peaches in heavy
  syrup
1/2 cup chopped onion
1/2 cup rice wine vinegar
1/4 cup sugar

1/4 teaspoon salt, or to taste
1/2 teaspoon ground cinnamon
1/4 teaspoon ground cloves
1/4 teaspoon ground allspice
1/4 teaspoon cayenne

DRAIN the peaches, reserving the syrup. CHOP the peaches coarsely. PLACE the reserved syrup in a medium saucepan. COOK over medium-high heat until reduced by half, stirring frequently. ADD the chopped peaches, onion, vinegar, sugar, salt, cinnamon, cloves, allspice and cayenne. BRING to a boil. COOK for 45 minutes or until thickened, stirring frequently. REMOVE from the heat. COOL for 15 minutes. PROCESS in a food processor until smooth. POUR into a container with a cover. CHILL, covered, for 8 to 12 hours to blend the flavors. SERVE with chicken or pork.

Kelton House Cranberry Relish

YIELD: 2 TO 3 CUPS

1 (16-ounce) package fresh
  cranberries, frozen
2 medium Granny Smith apples,
  peeled, cut into quarters

³/4 cup sugar
¹/2 cup sweet orange marmalade
2 tablespoons apricot brandy
¹/4 teaspoon ground cinnamon

RINSE the cranberries, discarding any stems. PROCESS in a food processor until coarsely chopped. PLACE in a medium bowl. CHOP the apples to the same size as the cranberries. ADD to the cranberries. ADD the sugar, orange marmalade, apricot brandy and cinnamon and mix well. CHILL, covered, in the refrigerator for 4 hours or up to several days.

Italian Relish

YIELD: ABOUT 2 CUPS

8 ounces pitted kalamata olives
8 ounces pitted green olives
1 large red bell pepper, cut into 6 to
  8 pieces
²/3 cup chopped olive oil-pack
  sun-dried tomatoes
2 tablespoons chopped fresh flat-leaf
  parsley leaves

3 garlic cloves, chopped
1 tablespoon chopped fresh oregano
  leaves
¹/3 cup olive oil
2 tablespoons red wine vinegar
1 tablespoon balsamic vinegar
¹/2 teaspoon freshly ground pepper

PROCESS the kalamata olives, green olives, red pepper and sun-dried tomatoes in a food processor until chunky. COMBINE with the parsley, garlic, oregano, olive oil, red wine vinegar, balsamic vinegar and pepper in a heavy saucepan. BRING to a boil. PACK into hot sterilized jars, leaving ¹/2 inch headspace. SEAL with 2-piece lids. PROCESS in a boiling water bath for 10 minutes.

NOTE: Serve on sandwiches or as an appetizer on baguettes cut and spread with butter or a little chèvre.

Brunch and Breads

MENU

MARINATED STEAK SALAD – *PAGE 46*

CHEESE FONDUE CASSEROLE – *PAGE 122*

DATE AND OATMEAL YOGURT MUFFINS – *PAGE 132*

PUMPKIN MUFFINS – *PAGE 133*

DOUBLE CHOCOLATE CAKE WITH CHOCOLATE GANACHE – *PAGE 146*

KEY LIMELIGHT PIE – *PAGE 164*

DOC'S BLOODY MARYS – *PAGE 41*

THE NORTH MARKET

This popular common market offers the chance for neighbors to gather and mingle while shopping for groceries, fresh flowers, and hard-to-find essentials that you won't find in any supermarket. Since 1876, North Market merchants have offered the finest meats, produce, poultry, seafood, grocery items, and prepared foods. In addition to the 35 merchants, the North Market hosts the city's largest outdoor Farmer's Market every Saturday from late April through December. Located on Spruce Street, the North Market has grown with the community while maintaining the qualities unique to a historic public market.

Savory Breakfast Casserole

YIELD: 10 TO 12 SERVINGS

2¹/₂ cups seasoned croutons
1 pound sausage
1 (10-ounce) package frozen chopped
    spinach, thawed
4 eggs
2¹/₄ cups milk
1 (10-ounce) can cream of mushroom
    soup

1 (4-ounce) can mushrooms, drained,
    chopped
1 cup shredded Cheddar cheese
    (4 ounces)
1 cup shredded Monterey Jack cheese
    (4 ounces)
¹/₄ teaspoon dry mustard

SPREAD the croutons in a greased 9x13-inch baking dish. BROWN the sausage in a skillet over medium heat, stirring until crumbly; drain. SPREAD over the croutons. DRAIN the spinach, squeezing out any excess liquid. WHISK the eggs and milk in a large bowl until blended. STIR in the soup, spinach, mushrooms, Cheddar cheese, Monterey Jack cheese and dry mustard. POUR over the sausage. CHILL, covered, for 8 to 12 hours. BAKE, uncovered, at 325 degrees for 50 to 55 minutes or until set and light brown on top.

Cheese Fondue Casserole

YIELD: 6 SERVINGS

1¹/₂ long loaves French bread
¹/₂ to 1 cup prepared mustard
1¹/₂ pounds Cheddar cheese, cut into
    ¹/₄-inch slices
4 eggs, beaten

5 cups milk
1¹/₂ teaspoons Worcestershire sauce
1 teaspoon salt
¹/₈ teaspoon cayenne
¹/₄ teaspoon paprika

CUT the bread into ¹/₂-inch slices. SPREAD 1 side generously with mustard. ALTERNATE layers of bread and cheese slices in a 4-quart baking dish. COMBINE the eggs, milk, Worcestershire sauce, salt and cayenne in a bowl and beat well. POUR over the layers in the baking dish. SPRINKLE the top with paprika. CHILL, covered, for 8 to 12 hours. BAKE, uncovered, at 350 degrees for 1¹/₂ hours or until the middle is cooked through and has puffed out over the top.

Zesty Brunch Enchiladas

YIELD: 8 SERVINGS

2 cups ground cooked ham
2¹/₂ cups shredded Cheddar cheese
¹/₂ cup sliced green onions
1 (4-ounce) can chopped green chiles, drained
8 (7-inch) flour tortillas

Cornmeal
4 eggs, beaten
2 cups light cream or milk
1 tablespoon flour
¹/₄ teaspoon garlic powder
Few drops of Tabasco sauce

COMBINE the ham, 1¹/₂ cups of the Cheddar cheese, green onions and green chiles in a bowl and mix well. PLACE ¹/₃ cup of the ham mixture at the end of each tortilla. ROLL up to enclose the ham mixture. ARRANGE seam side down in a greased and cornmeal-sprinkled 9x13-inch baking dish. COMBINE the eggs, cream, flour, garlic powder and Tabasco sauce in a bowl and mix well. POUR over the enchiladas. CHILL, covered, for 4 to 12 hours. BAKE, covered, at 350 degrees for 55 to 60 minutes or until set. SPRINKLE with the remaining 1 cup cheese. LET stand for 10 minutes before serving.

Gruyère and Shallot Quiches

YIELD: 12 SERVINGS

¹/₂ cup minced shallots
¹/₂ cup dry white wine
6 eggs
1 teaspoon salt

¹/₄ teaspoon white pepper
3 cups heavy cream
12 ounces grated Gruyère cheese
2 (8-ounce) pie shells, partially baked

BRING the shallots and wine to a boil in a skillet. REDUCE the heat. SIMMER for 2 minutes. REMOVE from heat. LET stand until cool. BEAT the eggs lightly in a bowl. ADD the shallot mixture, salt, white pepper and cream and mix well. SPRINKLE the cheese into each pie shell. POUR the egg mixture over the cheese. BAKE at 375 degrees for 25 to 35 minutes or until golden brown and firm in the center. REMOVE from the oven. LET stand for 5 to 10 minutes before serving.

Salmon Quiche

YIELD: 6 SERVINGS

1 cup whole wheat flour
2/3 cup shredded sharp Cheddar cheese
1/4 cup chopped almonds
1/2 teaspoon salt
1/4 teaspoon paprika
6 tablespoons vegetable oil
1 (15-ounce) can sockeye salmon
3 eggs, beaten
1 cup sour cream
1/4 cup mayonnaise
1/2 cup shredded sharp Cheddar cheese
1 tablespoon grated onion
1/4 teapoon dried dill
3 dashes of Tabasco sauce
Sprigs of fresh dill

COMBINE the whole wheat flour, 2/3 cup cheese, almonds, salt and paprika in a bowl and mix well. ADD the vegetable oil and mix well. RESERVE a small portion of the mixture. PRESS the remaining mixture in a 9-inch pie plate. BAKE at 400 degrees for 10 minutes. REMOVE from the oven. REDUCE the oven temperature to 325 degrees. DRAIN the salmon, reserving the liquid. ADD enough water to the reserved liquid to measure 1/2 cup. FLAKE the salmon in a bowl, discarding the skin and bones. COMBINE the eggs, sour cream, mayonnaise and reserved salmon liquid in a bowl and blend well. STIR in the salmon, 1/2 cup cheese, onion, dill and Tabasco sauce. SPOON into the prepared pie plate. SPRINKLE with the reserved flour mixture. BAKE for 45 minutes or until set. GARNISH with dill sprigs.

NOTE: Can use low-fat sour cream and mayonnaise in this recipe.

Easy Apple Coffee Cake

YIELD: 12 TO 16 SERVINGS

1 (21-ounce) can apple pie filling
1 (2-layer) package spice cake mix
3 eggs
2 tablespoons water
$1/2$ cup chopped pecans

$1/2$ cup raisins
$1/2$ cup packed brown sugar
$1/2$ cup flour
$1/2$ teaspoon ground cinnamon
$1/4$ cup butter, softened

COMBINE the pie filling, cake mix, eggs and water in a bowl and mix well. STIR in the pecans and raisins. SPOON into a greased and floured 9x13-inch baking pan. MIX the brown sugar, flour and cinnamon in a bowl. CUT in the butter until crumbly. SPRINKLE over the batter. BAKE at 350 degrees for 40 to 45 minutes or until the coffee cake tests done.

Blueberry Sour Cream Tea Ring

YIELD: 12 SERVINGS

$1/4$ cup packed brown sugar
$1/4$ cup chopped pecans
$1/2$ teaspoon ground cinnamon
1 (2-layer) package Duncan Hines®
   blueberry muffin mix

$3/4$ cup sour cream
1 egg
2 tablespoons water
$1/2$ cup confectioners' sugar
1 tablespoon milk

MIX the brown sugar, pecans and cinnamon in a bowl. RINSE the blueberries from the muffin mix with cold water and drain. COMBINE the muffin mix, sour cream, egg and water in a bowl and stir to mix well. POUR $1/3$ of the batter into a greased 7-cup tube pan. LAYER the brown sugar mixture, blueberries and remaining batter $1/2$ at a time in the prepared pan, ending with the batter. BAKE at 350 degrees for 33 to 37 minutes or until a wooden pick inserted in the center comes out clean. COOL in the pan for 10 minutes. INVERT onto a wire rack and turn right side up. COMBINE the confectioners' sugar and milk in a bowl and stir until smooth. DRIZZLE over the warm coffee cake on a serving plate.

SPECIAL thanks to Duncan Hines® for donating this recipe.

Night-Before French Toast Casserole

YIELD: 8 SERVINGS

Old-Fashioned Oatmeal Pancakes

YIELD: 6 TO 8 SERVINGS

8 (1¼-inch) slices Italian or
   French bread
8 eggs
3 cups milk

4 teaspoons sugar
1 teaspoon salt
1 tablespoon vanilla extract
2 tablespoons margarine

ARRANGE the sliced bread in a greased 9x13-inch baking pan. BEAT the eggs in a large bowl. ADD the milk, sugar, salt and vanilla and mix well. POUR over the bread. CHILL, covered, for 4 to 36 hours. UNCOVER and dot with the margarine. BAKE at 350 degrees for 45 to 50 minutes or until puffy and light brown. LET stand for 5 minutes before serving. SERVE with syrup or yogurt, honey, sour cream and fresh fruit.

2 cups rolled oats
2 cups buttermilk
½ cup flour
2 tablespoons sugar
1 teaspoon baking powder
1 teaspoon baking soda

½ teaspoon ground cinnamon
¼ teaspoon salt
2 eggs
¼ cup melted butter
½ cup grated apples or raisins
   (optional)

COMBINE the rolled oats and buttermilk in a bowl and mix well. CHILL, covered, in the refrigerator for 8 to 12 hours. SIFT the flour, sugar, baking powder, baking soda, cinnamon and salt together. BEAT the eggs lightly in a large bowl. ADD the butter and apples and mix well. STIR in the oat mixture. ADD the flour mixture and mix well. SPOON the batter by ¼ cupfuls onto a hot greased griddle, spreading into 4-inch circles. BAKE over medium heat until golden brown on each side, turning once.

Finnish Pancake

YIELD: 6 TO 8 SERVINGS

6 eggs
1 cup milk
1/4 cup orange juice
1/2 cup sugar

1 cup flour
1/4 teaspoon salt
1/2 cup unsalted butter
Confectioners' sugar

COMBINE the eggs, milk, orange juice, sugar, flour and salt in a food processor container fitted with a steel blade. PROCESS until well blended. PLACE the butter in a 9x13-inch baking dish. BAKE at 425 degrees until the butter is sizzling but not brown. REMOVE from the oven. POUR the batter into the hot butter. BAKE for 20 minutes or until puffed and brown. SPRINKLE with confectioners' sugar.

Chili Pecan Biscuits

YIELD: 12 TO 14 BISCUITS

1 3/4 cups flour
1/4 cup cornstarch
2 teaspoons baking powder
1 teaspoon baking soda
1/4 teaspoon salt
1/4 to 1/2 teaspoon chili powder
1/2 cup toasted chopped pecans

2 tablespoons finely chopped shallots
    or green onions
1 egg
1/3 cup heavy cream
1/2 cup buttermilk
1/4 cup melted unsalted butter

SIFT the flour, cornstarch, baking powder, baking soda, salt and chili powder into a large bowl. STIR in the pecans and shallots. WHISK the egg, cream, buttermilk and cooled melted butter in a small bowl until well blended. STIR into the flour mixture, adding additional buttermilk if needed. TURN onto a floured towel. PAT into a circle 1/2 inch thick. CUT into circles with a 2- to 2 1/2-inch biscuit cutter. PLACE on an ungreased baking sheet. BRUSH the tops with additional cream and sprinkle with additional chili powder. BAKE at 425 degrees for 12 to 15 minutes or until golden brown.

Cinnamon Rolls

YIELD: 1½ TO 2 DOZEN

2 tablespoons sugar
1½ teaspoons salt
¼ cup margarine
½ cup milk, scalded
1 envelope dry yeast
½ cup warm water
3 cups flour

1 egg
2 tablespoons water
¼ cup melted margarine
1 cup packed brown sugar
1 tablespoon ground cinnamon
Buttercream Frosting

COMBINE the sugar, salt and ¼ cup margarine in a bowl. ADD the scalded milk. COOL until lukewarm. DISSOLVE the yeast in the ½ cup warm water. ADD the yeast mixture, 1½ cups of the flour, egg and 2 tablespoons water to the milk mixture and beat until smooth. MIX in the remaining flour. LET rise for 3 to 4 hours or until doubled in bulk. ROLL the dough into a ½-inch-thick rectangle on a lightly floured surface. BRUSH with ¼ cup margarine, leaving 1 long end unbrushed. SPRINKLE with a mixture of brown sugar and cinnamon. ROLL as for a jelly roll and press to secure. CUT into 2-inch slices. PLACE in a greased 9x13-inch baking pan. LET rise for 8 to 12 hours or until doubled in bulk. BAKE at 400 degrees for 12 to 15 minutes or until golden brown. SPREAD with the Buttercream Frosting while warm.

BUTTERCREAM FROSTING

2 cups confectioners' sugar
¼ cup margarine, softened

½ teaspoon vanilla extract
1 tablespoon plus 1 teaspoon milk

BEAT the confectioners' sugar, margarine, vanilla and milk in a bowl until smooth. ADD additional milk if needed for the desired spreading consistency.

Herbed Spoon Rolls

YIELD: 2 DOZEN

1 envelope dry yeast
2 cups warm water
3/4 cup unsalted butter
1/4 cup sugar
1 egg

1/2 teaspoon salt
1 to 2 garlic cloves, minced
2 tablespoons minced fresh thyme or
    oregano
4 cups self-rising flour

DISSOLVE the yeast in the warm water. CREAM the butter and sugar in a mixer bowl until light and fluffy. ADD the egg and beat well. ADD the yeast and mix well. STIR in the salt, garlic and thyme. ADD the flour and mix well. CHILL, covered, in the refrigerator until ready to use. SPOON the batter into well greased muffin cups. BAKE at 350 degrees for 20 minutes or until golden brown.

Honey White Bread

YIELD: 1 LOAF

3 1/2 cups unbleached flour or bread
    flour
1 envelope dry yeast
1 teaspoon salt

1/4 cup vegetable oil
1/4 cup honey
1 cup hot (105 to 115 degrees) water

COMBINE the flour, yeast and salt in a food processor container. ADD the vegetable oil, honey and water. PROCESS for 1 minute or until the mixture forms a ball. PLACE in a greased bowl, turning to coat the surface. LET rise, covered, in a warm place for 1 to 1 1/2 hours or until doubled in bulk. PUNCH down the dough. SHAPE into a loaf. PLACE in a greased 5x8-inch loaf pan. LET rise in a warm place for 45 minutes or until doubled in bulk. BAKE at 375 degrees for 30 to 35 minutes or until golden brown. INVERT onto a wire rack to cool.

Apricot Nut Bread

YIELD: 1 LOAF

1 (12-ounce) can apricot nectar
³/₄ cup chopped dried apricots
³/₄ cup raisins
2 cups sifted flour
1 teaspoon baking soda
¹/₂ teaspoon salt

1 egg, beaten
1 cup sugar
1 tablespoon melted butter
¹/₃ cup milk
¹/₂ cup slivered almonds

COMBINE the nectar, apricots and raisins in a small saucepan. BRING to a boil and reduce the heat. SIMMER for 5 minutes. REMOVE from the heat. LET stand until cool. SIFT the flour, baking soda and salt together. BEAT the egg, sugar and butter in a bowl until smooth. ADD the flour mixture alternately with the milk, stirring constantly. FOLD in the fruit mixture and almonds. SPOON into a greased and floured 5x9-inch loaf pan. BAKE at 350 degrees for 1 hour or until the loaf tests done.

Banana Split Bread

YIELD: 1 LOAF

2 cups flour
1 teaspoon baking powder
¹/₂ teaspoon baking soda
1 cup mashed ripe bananas
3 tablespoons milk
1 cup sugar

1 egg
¹/₂ cup unsalted butter, softened
1 cup semisweet chocolate chips
¹/₂ cup chopped pecans
³/₄ cup chopped maraschino cherries

SIFT the flour, baking powder and baking soda together. MIX the bananas and milk in a small bowl. BEAT the sugar, egg and butter in a mixer bowl for 3 minutes or until light and fluffy. ADD the flour mixture and banana mixture alternately, stirring constantly until blended after each addition. STIR in the chocolate chips, pecans and maraschino cherries. SPOON into a greased and floured 5x9-inch loaf pan. BAKE at 350 degrees for 1 hour or until the loaf tests done. INVERT onto a wire rack. Cool for 10 minutes before serving.

Cranberry Bread

YIELD: 1 LOAF

2 cups flour
1 cup sugar
1½ teaspoons baking powder
½ teaspoon baking soda
½ teaspoon salt

1½ cups fresh cranberries
1 cup chopped walnuts
¾ cup orange juice
2 tablespoons shortening
1 egg, lightly beaten

SIFT the flour, sugar, baking powder, baking soda and salt into a large bowl. ADD the cranberries and walnuts and stir to coat well. HEAT the orange juice in a small saucepan. ADD the shortening and stir until melted. ADD to the flour mixture and mix well. BEAT in the egg. SPOON into a well greased 5x9-inch loaf pan. BAKE at 350 degrees for 1 hour. INVERT onto a wire rack to cool.

Peanut Butter Bread with Strawberry Butter

YIELD: 12 SERVINGS

2 cups flour
2 teaspoons baking powder
½ cup peanut butter
1 cup sugar
1 egg
1 teaspoon salt

1 cup milk
½ cup unsalted butter, softened
⅓ cup strawberry jam
Fresh lemon juice to taste
½ teaspoon sugar, or to taste

MIX the flour and baking powder together. BEAT the peanut butter, 1 cup sugar, egg and salt in a mixer bowl until smooth. ADD the flour mixture and milk alternately, mixing well after each addition. SPOON into a greased 5x9-inch loaf pan. BAKE at 350 degrees for 60 to 70 minutes or until the loaf tests done. BEAT the butter, jam, lemon juice and ½ teaspoon sugar in a mixer bowl until smooth and creamy. SERVE with the sliced bread.

Date and Oatmeal Yogurt Muffins

YIELD: 6 MUFFINS

Morning Glory Muffins

YIELD: 15 MUFFINS

$^3/_4$ cup flour
$^3/_4$ cup old-fashioned rolled oats
$^1/_4$ cup packed dark brown sugar
$1^1/_2$ teaspoons baking powder
$^1/_2$ teaspoon salt
$^1/_8$ teaspoon ground cinnamon
$^1/_3$ cup chopped pitted dried dates

$^1/_3$ cup walnut halves, lightly toasted, finely chopped
$^1/_2$ cup plain yogurt
$^1/_4$ cup milk
2 tablespoons melted unsalted butter
1 egg, lightly beaten

MIX the flour, oats, brown sugar, baking powder, salt, cinnamon, dates and walnuts in a large bowl. WHISK the yogurt, milk, butter and egg in a bowl. ADD to the flour mixture and mix until just combined. POUR into greased muffin cups. BAKE at 400 degrees for 30 minutes or until the muffins test done.

$^1/_2$ cup raisins
2 cups flour
1 cup sugar
2 teaspoons baking soda
2 teaspoons ground cinnamon
$^1/_2$ teaspoon salt
2 cups grated carrots

1 large Granny Smith apple, peeled, minced
$^1/_2$ cup chopped pecans
$^1/_2$ cup sweetened shredded coconut
3 eggs
$^2/_3$ cup vegetable oil
2 teaspoons vanilla extract

SOAK the raisins in hot water for 30 minutes and drain well. MIX the flour, sugar, baking soda, cinnamon and salt in a bowl. STIR in the drained raisins, carrots, apple, pecans and coconut. BEAT the eggs, oil and vanilla in a small bowl. ADD to the flour mixture and mix until just combined. SPOON into nonstick muffin cups. BAKE at 350 degrees for 20 minutes or until the muffins test done.

NOTE: Can substitute prunes and Delicious apple for the raisins and Granny Smith apple.

Pineapple Muffins

YIELD: 1 DOZEN

1^2/$_3$ cups flour
2 teaspoons (scant) baking powder
^{1}/$_4$ cup butter or margarine
1 cup (scant) sugar

2 eggs
^{1}/$_2$ cup milk
1 cup drained crushed pineapple

MIX the flour and baking powder together. CREAM the butter and sugar in a mixer bowl until light and fluffy. BEAT in the eggs. ADD the flour mixture alternately with the milk, beating well after each addition. STIR in the pineapple. SPOON into well greased muffin cups. BAKE at 400 degrees for 30 minutes or until the muffins test done. COOL on a wire rack.

Pumpkin Muffins

YIELD: 2 DOZEN

1 (15-ounce) can pumpkin
^{2}/$_3$ cup vegetable oil
2 cups sugar
4 eggs, beaten
^{2}/$_3$ cup milk
3^1/$_3$ cups flour

2 teaspoons baking soda
1^1/$_2$ teaspoons salt
^{1}/$_2$ teaspoon baking powder
2 teaspoons pumpkin pie spice
12 ounces semisweet miniature
  chocolate chips

COMBINE the pumpkin, vegetable oil, sugar, eggs and milk in a large bowl and mix well. MIX the flour, baking soda, salt, baking powder, pumpkin pie spice and chocolate chips in a bowl. ADD to the pumpkin mixture and mix well. FILL greased muffin cups ^{2}/$_3$ full. BAKE at 350 degrees for 25 minutes or until the muffins test done.

Cheese Popovers

YIELD: 1 DOZEN

1 cup water
1/2 cup butter or margarine
1 cup flour

4 eggs
1/3 cup grated Parmesan cheese
1/2 teaspoon salt

BRING the water and butter to a boil in a saucepan. ADD the flour. COOK over medium heat until the mixture forms a ball, stirring constantly. REMOVE from the heat. COOL for 5 minutes. BEAT in the eggs 1 at a time. ADD the Parmesan cheese and salt and beat well. SPOON into well greased muffin cups, filling 2/3 full. BAKE at 375 degrees for 40 minutes. PRICK each puff with a knife. BAKE for 5 minutes longer.

Brandied Apple Butter

YIELD: 1 1/2 PINTS

6 cups homemade unsweetened
   applesauce
1/2 cup apple brandy or brandy
1 cup sugar

1/2 cup honey
1 tablespoon ground cinnamon
1/4 teaspoon ground cloves
1/4 teaspoon ground nutmeg

COMBINE the applesauce, brandy, sugar, honey, cinnamon, cloves and nutmeg in an ovenproof saucepan. COOK over medium heat until the mixture begins to thicken, stirring constantly. BAKE at 300 degrees until the mixture is a deep brown, stirring frequently. SPOON into hot sterilized jars, leaving 1/4 inch head-space; seal with 2-piece lids. PROCESS in a boiling water bath for 10 minutes.

Amish Peach Jam

YIELD: 1½ PINTS

4 cups chopped peeled peaches
1 teaspoon fresh lemon juice
1½ cups orange juice
Grated peel of 1 orange

1 (1-ounce) bottle maraschino
  cherries, drained, cut into quarters
1 package powdered light fruit pectin
3 cups sugar

COMBINE the peaches, lemon juice, orange juice, orange peel and maraschino cherries in a large saucepan and mix well. MIX the pectin and ³/₄ cup of the sugar in a bowl. ADD to the peach mixture. BRING to a boil over high heat, stirring constantly. ADD the remaining sugar. RETURN to a boil, stirring constantly. BOIL for 1 minute. REMOVE from the heat and skim off any foam. POUR into hot sterilized jars, leaving ¹/₄ inch headspace; seal with 2-piece lids. PROCESS in a boiling water bath for 10 minutes.

Microwave Pumpkin Butter

YIELD: 1½ PINTS

1 (28-ounce) can pumpkin
1 tablespoon pumpkin pie spice

1 package powdered fruit pectin
4¹/₂ cups sugar

COMBINE the pumpkin, pumpkin pie spice and pectin in a 3-quart microwave-safe dish and cover tightly. MICROWAVE on High for 5 minutes; stir. MICROWAVE for 5 to 6 minutes longer or until the mixture bubbles around the edge. STIR in the sugar. MICROWAVE, covered, on High for 5 minutes; stir. MICROWAVE for 5 minutes longer or until the mixture boils. MICROWAVE for 1 minute longer. SPOON into hot sterilized jars, leaving ¹/₄ inch headspace. PROCESS in a boiling water bath for 10 minutes.

Celebrated Endings

SWEET DREAMS

MENU

PUMPKIN CHEESECAKE WITH MAPLE PECAN GLAZE – *PAGE 139*

CARAMEL SOUFFLÉ – *PAGE 140*

LIME FOOL WITH STRAWBERRIES AND KIWIFRUIT – *PAGE 141*

CHOCOLATE MOUSSE TORTE – *PAGE 150*

HOLIDAY EGGNOG CAKE – *PAGE 153*

THE STATEHOUSE

The Statehouse complex represents one of America's finest examples of Greek Revival civic architecture and is one of the oldest working statehouses in the United States. A recent seven-year restoration has brought the statehouse back to its 1861 glory. Visitors can see where and how the vital business of state government is conducted, while at the same time viewing magnificent architectural and artistic treasures. The Statehouse Education and Visitors Center interprets the state capital's history and significance for the public, and guides school groups in their study of government, citizenship, and Ohio history.

Bananas Foster

YIELD: 2 SERVINGS

1 large banana
3 tablespoons brown sugar
2 tablespoons butter
1 teaspoon lemon juice
$^1/_8$ teaspoon ground cinnamon
2 tablespoons banana liqueur
2 ounces white rum

PEEL the banana and cut into halves lengthwise. SAUTÉ in the brown sugar and butter in a saucepan until tender. SPRINKLE with the lemon juice and cinnamon. ADD the liqueur and rum. REMOVE from the heat and ignite. BASTE the banana until the flames subside. SERVE over vanilla ice cream.

Fudge Truffle Cheesecake

YIELD: 16 SERVINGS

$1^1/_2$ cups vanilla wafer crumbs
$^1/_3$ cup baking cocoa
$^1/_2$ cup confectioners' sugar
$^1/_3$ cup melted butter or margarine
2 cups semisweet chocolate chips
24 ounces cream cheese, softened
1 (14-ounce) can sweetened
    condensed milk
4 eggs
2 teaspoons vanilla extract

COMBINE the vanilla wafer crumbs, baking cocoa, confectioners' sugar and butter in a bowl and mix well. PRESS into a 9-inch springform pan. MICROWAVE the chocolate chips in a glass bowl until melted. BEAT the cream cheese in a mixer bowl until light and fluffy. ADD the condensed milk gradually, beating until smooth. ADD the melted chocolate, eggs and vanilla and mix well. POUR into the prepared pan. POUR enough hot water into a 5x9-inch loaf pan to fill halfway. PLACE on the lower oven rack. PLACE the cheesecake on the middle oven rack above the hot water. BAKE at 300 degrees for 65 minutes or until the center is set. COOL completely before removing the side of the pan.

Pumpkin Cheesecake with Maple Pecan Glaze

YIELD: 16 SERVINGS

1¼ cups graham cracker crumbs
¼ cup melted butter
¼ cup sugar
24 ounces cream cheese, softened
1 (14-ounce) can sweetened
  condensed milk
1 (15-ounce) can pumpkin

3 eggs
¼ cup maple syrup
1½ teaspoons ground cinnamon
1 teaspoon grated nutmeg
½ teaspoon salt
Maple Pecan Glaze

MIX the graham cracker crumbs, butter and sugar in a bowl. PRESS into a 10-inch springform pan. BEAT the cream cheese in a mixer bowl until light and fluffy. ADD the condensed milk gradually, beating until smooth. ADD the pumpkin, eggs, maple syrup, cinnamon, nutmeg and salt and mix well. POUR into the prepared pan. BAKE at 300 degrees for 1¼ hours or until the edge springs back when lightly touched. COOL completely. SPREAD the Maple Pecan Glaze on top of the cooled cheesecake. CHILL in the refrigerator for 2 hours or longer. REMOVE the side of the pan before serving.

MAPLE PECAN GLAZE

¾ cup maple syrup
1 cup heavy cream

½ cup chopped pecans

COMBINE the maple syrup and cream in a medium saucepan. BRING to a boil. BOIL for 15 to 20 minutes or until thickened, stirring occasionally. STIR in the pecans.

Caramel Soufflé

YIELD: 4 TO 6 SERVINGS

2$^{1}/_{2}$ cups sugar
8 egg whites
$^{1}/_{2}$ teaspoon cream of tartar
$^{1}/_{8}$ teaspoon salt

PLACE 1$^{1}/_{4}$ cups of the sugar in a small heavy skillet. COOK over medium heat for 7 to 8 minutes or until the sugar melts and turns a caramel color, stirring constantly with a wooden spoon. POUR half of the caramel into a 2-quart soufflé dish, tilting so that the caramel covers the bottom of the dish. BEAT the egg whites, cream of tartar and salt in a mixer bowl until soft peaks form. ADD the remaining 1$^{1}/_{4}$ cups sugar gradually, beating constantly until stiff peaks form. REMELT the remaining caramel if needed. ADD to the stiffly beaten egg whites gradually and carefully along the side of the bowl, beating constantly. CONTINUE to beat for 5 minutes or until stiff peaks form. SPOON into the prepared soufflé dish. SET inside a large baking dish. FILL the large baking dish with enough hot water to come halfway up the side of the soufflé dish. SET on the lower oven rack. REMOVE the remaining oven racks because the soufflé will puff. BAKE at 300 degrees for 45 to 60 minutes or until the top is firm. SERVE warm or at room temperature.

NOTE: The soufflé will last for 3 to 4 hours without falling.

Lime Fool with Strawberries and Kiwifruit

YIELD: 4 SERVINGS

$1/4$ cup heavy cream
$1/4$ cup lime juice
1 teaspoon grated lime peel
6 ounces white chocolate
$3/4$ cup whipping cream
3 tablespoons sugar
2 cups strawberries, sliced
4 or 5 ripe kiwifruit, sliced
4 whole strawberries, cut into fans

BRING $1/4$ cup cream, lime juice and lime peel to a simmer in a heavy saucepan. REMOVE from the heat. ADD the white chocolate and stir until melted and smooth. CHILL for 25 minutes or until cool but not set. BEAT $3/4$ cup whipping cream in a mixer bowl until soft peaks form. ADD the sugar gradually, beating until stiff peaks form. FOLD into the lime mixture. PLACE a layer of sliced strawberries in clear wine, sherbet or champagne glasses. ARRANGE the kiwifruit slices against the side of the glasses above the strawberries. SPOON $1/3$ of the lime filling into each glass, making sure the kiwifruit slices remain against the side of the glass. LAYER remaining strawberries and lime filling over the top. CHILL, covered, for 2 hours or longer. GARNISH each with a fanned strawberry with a stem before serving.

Espresso Ice

YIELD: 3 CUPS

1/2 to 2/3 cup sugar, or to taste
3 cups hot strong brewed espresso

Whipped cream

DISSOLVE the sugar in the hot espresso in a pitcher. CHILL in the refrigerator. POUR into a flat-bottomed metal pan. PLACE the pan on a baking sheet and place in the freezer. FREEZE for 45 minutes or until frozen around the edges. BLEND the frozen and unfrozen espresso with 2 knives. FREEZE for 2 hours longer, repeating the blending process every 30 to 40 minutes or until all of the espresso is fully crystallized. SPOON or scrape the espresso into wine glasses and top with whipped cream.

Vodka and Grapefruit Sorbet

YIELD: 4 CUPS

1 1/3 cups water
2 cups sugar
1/2 cup vodka

2 cups strained freshly squeezed pink
or white grapefruit juice, chilled

COMBINE the water and sugar in a small saucepan. COOK over medium-high heat until the sugar dissolves, stirring constantly. POUR into a pitcher. CHILL in the refrigerator. COMBINE 2 cups of the chilled sugar syrup, vodka and grapefruit juice in a pitcher and mix well. POUR into a 9x13-inch pan. FREEZE for 3 to 4 hours or until partially frozen. BREAK up and stir the mixture. RETURN to the freezer. FREEZE until firm. PROCESS in a food processor until of the desired consistency before serving.

Almond Cake with Raspberry Sauce

YIELD: 12 SERVINGS

$^3/_4$ cup sugar
$^1/_2$ cup unsalted butter, softened
8 ounces almond paste
3 eggs
1 tablespoon kirsch, Triple Sec or
   Cointreau

$^1/_4$ teaspoon almond extract
$^1/_4$ cup flour
$^1/_3$ teaspoon baking powder
Confectioners' sugar
Raspberry Sauce

CREAM the sugar, butter and almond paste in a medium mixer bowl until light and fluffy. BEAT in the eggs, kirsch and almond extract. ADD a mixture of the flour and baking powder, beating just until mixed through. DO not overbeat. SPOON into a generously buttered and floured 8-inch round cake pan. BAKE at 350 degrees for 40 to 50 minutes or until a cake tester inserted in the center comes out clean. COOL on a wire rack. INVERT onto a serving plate. SPRINKLE lightly with confectioners' sugar. SERVE with the Raspberry Sauce.

RASPBERRY SAUCE

2 cups fresh raspberries

2 tablespoons sugar, or to taste

PURÉE the raspberries and sugar in a food processor. PRESS the sauce gently through a fine sieve and discard the seeds.

NOTE: Can substitute one 12-ounce package frozen raspberries, thawed and omit the sugar.

Banana Cake with Caramel Frosting

YIELD: 12 TO 16 SERVINGS

2 cups flour
1 teaspoon baking powder
1 teaspoon baking soda
1 cup melted butter
1¹/₄ cups sugar

2 eggs
2 bananas, sliced
1 teaspoon vanilla extract
1 cup buttermilk or sour milk
Caramel Frosting

SIFT the flour, baking powder and baking soda together. CREAM the butter and sugar in a mixer bowl until light and fluffy. ADD the eggs and beat well. ADD the bananas and vanilla and mix well. ADD the flour mixture and buttermilk alternately, beating well after each addition. SPOON into two greased and floured 8-inch round cake pans. BAKE at 350 degrees for 30 to 45 minutes or until the layers test done. COOL in the pans for several minutes. INVERT onto wire racks to cool completely. SPREAD the Caramel Frosting between the layers and over the top and side of the cake.

NOTE: To sour milk, add 1 tablespoon lemon juice or white vinegar to 70-degree milk. Let stand for about 10 minutes.

CARAMEL FROSTING

¹/₂ cup butter
1 cup packed brown sugar

¹/₄ cup milk
2 cups confectioners' sugar

MELT the butter in a saucepan. ADD the brown sugar. COOK over medium-high heat until bubbly. ADD the milk. RETURN to a simmer, stirring constantly until the sugar is dissolved. REMOVE from the heat. LET stand until cool. ADD the confectioners' sugar and beat until smooth and creamy.

Carrot Layer Cake

YIELD: 12 TO 16 SERVINGS

2 cups cake flour
2 teaspoons baking soda
1/2 teaspoon salt
1 teaspoon ground cinnamon
3 cups finely grated carrots
1 1/2 cups vegetable oil

4 eggs
2 cups sugar
1 teaspoon vanilla extract
1 cup chopped pecans
Cream Cheese Frosting
Pecan halves

MIX the cake flour, baking soda, salt and cinnamon together. COMBINE the carrots and vegetable oil in a mixer bowl. ADD the eggs and sugar. BEAT until well blended. STIR in the flour mixture. ADD the vanilla and chopped pecans and mix well. SPOON into 2 greased and floured 9-inch round cake pans. BAKE at 350 degrees for 40 to 45 minutes or until the layers test done. COOL in the pans for 10 minutes. INVERT onto wire racks to cool completely. SPREAD the Cream Cheese Frosting between the layers and over the top of the cake. GARNISH with pecan halves.

CREAM CHEESE FROSTING

8 ounces cream cheese, softened
1 (1-pound) package confectioners' sugar

Milk

BEAT the cream cheese in a mixer bowl until smooth. ADD the confectioners' sugar and mix well. ADD a small amount of milk if needed for the desired spreading consistency.

Double Chocolate Cake with Chocolate Ganache

YIELD: 8 TO 10 SERVINGS

1/2 cup plus 2 tablespoons flour
1 1/2 teaspoons baking powder
3/4 teaspoon baking soda
1/2 teaspoon salt
1/2 cup plus 2 tablespoons unsalted butter, softened
1 cup sugar
1/2 cup baking cocoa
1/2 cup water
4 eggs
Triple Sec
Chocolate Ganache

SIFT the flour, baking powder, baking soda and salt together. CREAM the butter and sugar in a mixer bowl until light and fluffy. ADD the baking cocoa and water. BEAT for 7 minutes. ADD the flour mixture. BEAT for 2 minutes. ADD the eggs. BEAT for 5 minutes. POUR into a greased and floured 9-inch round cake pan. BAKE at 350 degrees for 30 to 40 minutes or until set. INVERT onto a wire rack to cool. CUT the cake horizontally into 3 layers. DRIZZLE each layer with liqueur. BEAT the refrigerated Chocolate Ganache until light in color and holds its shape. PLACE 1 cake layer on a wire rack or 9-inch cardboard circle. SPREAD 1/2 of the beatened ganache over the layer. PLACE another cake layer on top. SPREAD with the remaining beatened ganache. TOP with the remaining cake layer. POUR the room temperature ganache carefully over the top to glaze. TRANSFER the cake to a serving platter using long spatulas.

CHOCOLATE GANACHE

18 ounces semisweet chocolate
1 1/2 cups heavy cream

MELT the chocolate in a double boiler over simmering water. STIR in the cream. DIVIDE the mixture into 2 portions. CHILL 1 portion in the refrigerator for 3 to 4 hours or until thick and creamy. LET the remaining portion stand at room temperature.

Milky Way Cake

YIELD: 12 TO 16 SERVINGS

1/2 cup butter
6 large Milky Way candy bars
2 1/2 cups flour
1/2 teaspoon baking soda
1/2 cup butter, softened

2 cups sugar
4 eggs
1 1/4 cups buttermilk
1 cup chopped pecans
Confectioners' sugar

MELT 1/2 cup butter and candy bars in a heavy saucepan, stirring constantly. MIX the flour and baking soda together. CREAM 1/2 cup butter and sugar in a mixer bowl until light and fluffy. ADD the eggs 1 at a time, beating well after each addition. BEAT in the candy bar mixture. ADD the flour mixture and buttermilk alternately, beating well after each addition. STIR in the pecans. POUR into a greased and floured bundt pan. BAKE at 325 degrees for 1 hour and 10 minutes. COOL in the pan for 10 minutes. INVERT onto a wire rack to cool completely. SPRINKLE with confectioners' sugar.

NOTE: This cake is very rich and can be cut into small slices for serving.

Milky Way Icing

2 cups packed brown sugar
2 tablespoons flour
1/4 cup plus 3 tablespoons milk
2 tablespoons butter

1 teaspoon vanilla extract
2 Milky Way candy bars, coarsely
   chopped

COMBINE the brown sugar, flour, milk, butter and vanilla in a heavy saucepan. BRING to a boil. BOIL for 1 minute, stirring constantly. ADD the candy. COOK until the candy is melted and the icing is of the desired spreading consistency, stirring constantly. USE to frost your favorite cake.

Sour Cream Chocolate Cake with Sour Cream Chocolate Frosting

YIELD: 8 TO 10 SERVINGS

2 cups cake flour
2 teaspoons baking powder
1 teaspoon baking soda
1/4 teaspoon salt
3 ounces unsweetened chocolate, chopped

1/2 cup warm water
3/4 cup unsalted butter, softened
1 3/4 cups sugar
3 eggs
1 cup sour cream
Sour Cream Chocolate Frosting

MIX the cake flour, baking powder, baking soda and salt together. BRING the chocolate and water to a boil in a saucepan. COOK until the chocolate is melted, stirring constantly. LET stand until cool. BEAT the butter and sugar in a mixer bowl until light and fluffy. BEAT in the eggs 1 at a time. BEAT in the sour cream and chocolate until smooth. STIR in the flour mixture. SPOON into 3 greased and floured 8-inch round cake pans. BAKE at 350 degrees for 35 minutes or until the layers test done. COOL in the pans on wire racks for 15 minutes. INVERT onto wire racks to cool completely. SPREAD Sour Cream Chocolate Frosting between the layers and over the top and side of cake.

SOUR CREAM CHOCOLATE FROSTING

3/4 cup unsalted butter
4 1/2 ounces unsweetened chocolate
3 cups confectioners' sugar

3 tablespoons baking cocoa
3/4 cup sour cream

MELT the butter and chocolate in a saucepan over low heat, stirring constantly. POUR into a large bowl. ADD 1 cup of the confectioners' sugar, baking cocoa and 1/2 of the sour cream and whisk until smooth. ADD enough of the remaining confectioners' sugar and remaining sour cream gradually, whisking constantly until of the desired spreading consistency.

Red Velvet Cake with Mock Whipped Frosting

YIELD: 12 TO 16 SERVINGS

2 tablespoons baking cocoa
2 ounces red food coloring
1 1/2 cups sugar
1/2 cup shortening
2 eggs
1/2 teaspoon salt

1 teaspoon vanilla extract
1 cup buttermilk
2 1/4 cups cake flour
1 tablespoon white wine vinegar
1 teaspoon baking soda
Mock Whipped Frosting

MIX the baking cocoa and red food coloring in a small bowl to form a paste. CREAM the sugar and shortening in a mixer bowl until light and fluffy. ADD the eggs and baking cocoa paste and mix well. STIR the salt and vanilla into the buttermilk. ADD alternately with the cake flour to the creamed mixture, beating well after each addition. MIX the vinegar and baking soda together. FOLD into the batter. DO not beat. SPOON into 2 greased and floured 9-inch round cake pans. BAKE at 350 degrees for 30 minutes or until the layers test done. COOL in the pans for a few minutes. INVERT onto wire racks to cool completely. CUT each layer horizontally into halves. SPREAD Mock Whipped Frosting between the layers and over the top and side of cake.

MOCK WHIPPED FROSTING

5 tablespoons flour, sifted
1 cup milk
1 cup butter, softened

1 cup sugar
1 teaspoon vanilla extract

COMBINE the flour and milk in a saucepan. COOK until thickened, stirring constantly. LET stand until cool. CREAM the butter and sugar in a mixer bowl until light and fluffy. BEAT in the vanilla. ADD to the cooled milk mixture, beating constantly. BEAT until the mixture is the consistency of whipped cream.

Chocolate Mousse Torte

YIELD: 12 TO 16 SERVINGS

$^1/_4$ cup sifted baking cocoa
$^1/_3$ cup boiling water
$^1/_4$ cup unsalted butter, softened
$^3/_4$ cup sugar
$^1/_8$ teaspoon salt
$^1/_2$ teaspoon vanilla extract
1 egg
$^1/_2$ teaspoon baking soda
$^1/_2$ cup sour cream
1 cup sifted flour
$^1/_4$ cup walnut pieces
Chocolate Mousse
Chocolate Glaze

MIX the baking cocoa and boiling water in a small bowl until smooth. BEAT the butter in a large mixer bowl until light and fluffy. ADD the sugar, salt and vanilla and beat well. BEAT in the egg until smooth. STIR the baking soda into the sour cream in a small bowl. ADD the flour and the sour cream mixture alternately $^1/_3$ at a time to the egg mixture, beating at low speed just until smooth after each addition and scraping the side of the bowl with a rubber spatula. ADD the baking cocoa mixture and beat only until smooth. STIR in the walnuts. POUR into a well greased and floured 10-inch springform pan. SHAKE the pan and rotate slightly to level the top. BAKE at 350 degrees for 25 to 30 minutes or until the cake barely begins to pull from the side of the pan. COOL in the pan for 1 hour. SPREAD the Chocolate Mousse over the cooled cake in the pan. LEVEL the top. FREEZE for 2 hours or until set. REMOVE the cake from the freezer. RUN a knife around the inside of the pan to loosen the cake from the side. REMOVE the side of the pan. PLACE the cake on a wire rack with a pan underneath. POUR the Chocolate Glaze over the top, allowing the glaze to run down the side of the cake. SMOOTH the Chocolate Glaze around the side with a palette knife.

Chocolate Mousse Torte

(CONTINUED)

CHOCOLATE MOUSSE

12 ounces semisweet chocolate
4 egg yolks
1 egg
1 teaspoon instant coffee
1½ cups whipping cream
3 tablespoons confectioners' sugar
4 egg whites

MELT the chocolate in a double boiler over simmering water. REMOVE from the heat. WHIP the egg yolks, egg and coffee powder in a bowl until light and creamy. BLEND in the melted chocolate. WHIP the cream and confectioners' sugar in a large mixer bowl until fairly firm peaks form. FOLD in the chocolate mixture. BEAT the egg whites at high speed in a mixer bowl until moist and fluffy. FOLD into the chocolate mixture.

CHOCOLATE GLAZE

3 ounces semisweet chocolate
3 tablespoons sugar
2 tablespoons water
2 tablespoons unsalted butter, softened

BREAK up the chocolate and place in a small double boiler. ADD the sugar and water. COOK over hot water over medium heat until smooth, stirring occasionally. REMOVE the pan from over the hot water. ADD the butter and stir until smooth. LET stand at room temperature until slightly thickened, stirring occasionally.

151

Mocha Chocolate Torte

YIELD: 16 SERVINGS

8 ounces semisweet chocolate
8 ounces unsalted butter
$1/2$ cup sugar
$1/2$ cup very strong brewed coffee or espresso
4 eggs, at room temperature
Confectioners' sugar
Fresh whole raspberries
Fresh whole strawberries

COVER the bottom of a 9-inch springform pan with foil. SPRAY the bottom and side with nonstick cooking spray. COMBINE the chocolate, butter, sugar and brewed coffee in a heavy saucepan. COOK over low heat until smooth, stirring occasionally. REMOVE from the heat. BEAT the eggs in a mixer bowl for 2 minutes or until thick and pale yellow. ADD the chocolate mixture and beat until blended. POUR into the prepared pan. BAKE at 350 degrees for 30 to 35 minutes or until the top begins to crack slightly. REMOVE from the oven and cover with foil. CHILL for 3 to 12 hours before serving. UNCOVER and remove the side of the pan. SPRINKLE with confectioners' sugar. GARNISH with raspberries and strawberries.

NOTE: Can substitute $1/2$ cup Bailey's Irish Cream or $1/2$ cup Kahlúa for the brewed coffee.

Holiday Eggnog Cake

YIELD: 12 TO 16 SERVINGS

2 cups flour
1½ cups sugar
3½ teaspoons baking powder
2 teaspoons salt
1 teaspoon ground nutmeg
¼ teaspoon ground ginger

¼ cup shortening
¼ cup butter or margarine, softened
1 cup eggnog
1 teaspoon rum extract
3 eggs
Eggnog Fluff

COMBINE the flour, sugar, baking powder, salt, nutmeg, ginger, shortening, butter, eggnog, rum extract and eggs in a large mixer bowl. BEAT at medium speed for 30 seconds, scraping the bowl constantly. BEAT at high speed for 3 minutes, scraping the bowl occasionally. POUR into 2 greased and floured 8-inch round cake pans. BAKE at 350 degrees for 30 to 35 minutes or until a wooden pick inserted in the center of the layers comes out clean. COOL in the pans for 10 minutes. INVERT onto wire racks to cool completely. SPREAD the Eggnog Fluff between the layers and over the top and side of cake.

NOTE: Can bake in a greased and floured 9x13-inch cake pan for 40 to 45 minutes or until the cake tests done.

EGGNOG FLUFF

1½ cups whipping cream
½ cup confectioners' sugar

1 teaspoon rum extract

POUR the whipping cream into a chilled medium mixer bowl. ADD the confectioners' sugar and rum extract and beat until stiff peaks form.

Gingerbread

YIELD: 8 TO 12 SERVINGS

2 1/2 cups flour
1 cup sugar
Salt to taste
1 teaspoon ground ginger
1/2 teaspoon ground allspice
1/2 cup butter or margarine

2 tablespoons treacle or molasses
1 cup milk
1 teaspoon baking soda
1 egg, beaten
Fruit Compote Sauce (page 166)

SIFT the flour, sugar, salt, ginger and allspice into a bowl. COMBINE the butter, treacle and 1/4 cup of the milk in a saucepan. HEAT until the butter is melted, stirring constantly. ADD to the flour mixture and mix well. DISSOLVE the baking soda in the remaining milk. ADD with the beaten egg to the batter. BEAT until smooth. SPOON into a nonstick cake pan. BAKE at 350 degrees for 30 minutes. REDUCE the oven temperature to 325 degrees. BAKE for 45 to 60 minutes longer or until the gingerbread tests done. SERVE with Fruit Compote Sauce.

Cappuccino Bonbons

YIELD: 40 BONBONS

1 family-size package Duncan Hines® chewy fudge brownie mix
2 eggs
1/3 cup water
1/3 cup Crisco® oil

1 1/2 tablespoons Folgers® instant coffee
1 teaspoon ground cinnamon
Whipped topping
Ground cinnamon to taste

PLACE forty 2-inch foil cupcake liners on baking sheets. COMBINE the brownie mix, eggs, water, oil, coffee powder and 1 teaspoon cinnamon in a bowl. STIR for 50 strokes or until blended. FILL each cupcake liner with 1 tablespoonful of batter. BAKE at 350 degrees for 12 to 15 minutes or until a wooden pick inserted into the center comes out clean. COOL completely. CHILL until ready to serve. GARNISH with whipped topping and a dash of cinnamon.

Special thanks to Duncan Hines® for their generous support.

Square Buckeyes

YIELD: 3 DOZEN

1 cup margarine
1 cup peanut butter
1 (1-pound) package confectioners'
  sugar

2 cups semisweet chocolate chips
1/2 cup peanut butter

MELT the margarine and 1 cup peanut butter in a saucepan, stirring constantly. STIR in the confectioners' sugar. SPREAD in a 9x13-inch pan. MELT the chocolate chips and 1/2 cup peanut butter in a saucepan, stirring constantly. SPREAD over the top. CHILL until firm. CUT into squares.

White Chocolate Brittle

YIELD: ABOUT 2 POUNDS

2 cups white chocolate chips
1 cup broken pretzel sticks
1 cup cocktail peanuts

1 cup miniature marshmallows
  (optional)

MICROWAVE the white chocolate chips in a microwave-safe dish for 2 minutes or until melted. STIR in the pretzel sticks, peanuts and marshmallows. SPREAD on a greased baking sheet. LET stand until firm. BREAK into pieces. STORE in an airtight container.

Sweet Clouds

YIELD: 5 TO 6 DOZEN

2 pounds white chocolate
1 cup chunky peanut butter
2 cups miniature marshmallows
2 cups dry roasted peanuts
2 cups crisp rice cereal

MELT the white chocolate in a double boiler over hot water. STIR in the peanut butter. ADD the marshmallows, peanuts and cereal and mix well. DROP by rounded teaspoonfuls 1 inch apart onto waxed paper. LET stand until firm.

Anise Biscotti

YIELD: 3 TO 4 DOZEN

5 cups flour
1¹/₃ cups sugar
2 tablespoons baking powder
³/₄ cup butter
¹/₂ cup shortening
2 tablespoons plus 2 teaspoons anise seeds
1 (1-ounce) bottle of anise flavoring
5 eggs, beaten

COMBINE the flour, sugar and baking powder in a large bowl. CUT in the butter and shortening until crumbly. ADD the anise seeds and mix well. ADD the anise flavoring and eggs and mix well to form a soft dough using hands. DIVIDE the dough into 4 portions. ROLL each portion 3 inches wide. PLACE 2 portions each on greased cookie sheets. BAKE at 350 degrees for 15 to 20 minutes or until brown. REMOVE from the cookie sheets carefully and cut each diagonally into slices. RETURN to the cookie sheets. BAKE for 10 minutes on each side. REMOVE to wire racks to cool.

Orange and Cinnamon Biscotti

YIELD: ABOUT 2 DOZEN

2 cups flour
1½ teaspoons baking powder
1 teaspoon ground cinnamon
¼ teaspoon salt
½ cup unsalted butter, softened
1 cup sugar
2 eggs
2 teaspoons grated orange peel
1 teaspoon vanilla extract

MIX the flour, baking powder, cinnamon and salt together. CREAM the butter and sugar in a mixer bowl until light and fluffy. ADD the eggs 1 at a time, beating well after each addition. BEAT in the orange peel and vanilla. ADD the flour mixture and mix well. DIVIDE the dough into 2 portions. ROLL each portion 3 inches wide and ¾ inch thick. PLACE on 2 greased cookie sheets. BAKE at 325 degrees for 35 minutes or until firm. REMOVE to a cutting board. CUT diagonally into ½-inch thick slices using a serrated knife. ARRANGE cut side down on the cookie sheets. BAKE until both sides are golden brown, turning once.

White Chocolate Brownies

YIELD: 18 SERVINGS

1 cup unsalted butter
10 ounces white chocolate, broken
    into small pieces
1¼ cups sugar
4 eggs

1 tablespoon vanilla extract
2 cups flour
½ teaspoon salt
1 cup chopped pecan halves

LINE a 9x13-inch baking pan with foil, leaving an overhang around the edges. BUTTER the foil. HEAT the butter and white chocolate in a saucepan until melted, stirring constantly. COOL slightly. STIR in the sugar using a wooden spoon. STIR in the eggs and vanilla; the mixture will look curdled. ADD the flour, salt and pecans and stir quickly until just mixed. POUR into the prepared pan. BAKE at 325 degrees for 30 to 35 minutes or until the top is golden brown and the center is still soft when pressed lightly. LET stand until cool. CHILL for 3 hours or longer. LIFT the brownies from the pan using the foil overhang. CUT into squares.

Chocolate Cranberry Cookies

YIELD: ABOUT 2 DOZEN

½ cup butter, softened
1 cup flour
¾ cup sugar
1 egg
1 teaspoon vanilla extract

½ teaspoon baking powder
1 cup rolled oats
1 cup chopped cranberries
2 dozen (about) chocolate kiss candies

BEAT the butter in a mixer bowl until creamy. ADD the flour, sugar, egg, vanilla and baking powder and mix well. STIR in the oats and cranberries. DROP by rounded teaspoonfuls onto nonstick cookie sheets. PLACE a candy in the center of each. BAKE at 375 degrees for 10 to 12 minutes or until golden brown. COOL on a wire rack.

Chocolate Mint Squares

YIELD: 20 SERVINGS

1 cup sugar
$^1/_2$ cup margarine, softened
4 eggs
1 cup flour
1 teaspoon salt
1 teaspoon vanilla extract
1 (16-ounce) can chocolate syrup
$2^1/_2$ cups confectioners' sugar
$^1/_4$ cup plus 2 tablespoons crème de menthe
$^3/_4$ cup margarine, softened
2 cups chocolate chips
$^1/_2$ cup butter

CREAM the sugar and $^1/_2$ cup margarine in a mixer bowl until light and fluffy. ADD the eggs, flour, salt, vanilla and chocolate syrup and beat well. POUR into a greased 10x15-inch baking pan. BAKE at 350 degrees for 25 to 30 minutes or until the edges pull from the sides of the pan. LET stand until cool. COMBINE the confectioners' sugar, crème de menthe and $^3/_4$ cup margarine in a mixer bowl and beat until smooth. SPREAD over the cool layer. MELT the chocolate chips and $^1/_2$ cup butter in a saucepan. SPREAD over the crème de menthe layer. LET stand until set. CUT into squares.

Old-Fashioned Lemon Bars

YIELD: 2 DOZEN

1 cup butter, softened
½ cup confectioners' sugar
2 cups flour
4 eggs, beaten
2 cups sugar
Grated peel of 2 lemons

¼ cup fresh lemon juice
¼ cup flour
1 teaspoon baking powder
Creamy Frosting
Fresh mint leaves

CREAM the butter and confectioners' sugar in a mixer bowl until light and fluffy. STIR in 2 cups flour. PRESS into a nonstick 9x13-inch baking pan. BAKE at 350 degrees for 20 minutes or until golden brown. COMBINE the eggs, sugar, lemon peel and lemon juice in a bowl and mix well. SIFT ¼ cup flour and baking powder together. STIR into the egg mixture. POUR over the hot crust. BAKE for 20 to 25 minutes or until the filling is set. LET stand until cool. SPREAD the Creamy Frosting over the top. CUT into small bars. GARNISH bars with fresh mint leaves.

CREAMY FROSTING

3 tablespoons butter, softened
2 tablespoons heavy cream

1 teaspoon vanilla or lemon extract
1 to 2 cups confectioners' sugar

BEAT the butter, cream and vanilla in a mixer bowl until smooth. ADD the confectioners' sugar gradually, beating until of the desired spreading consistency.

Pecan Squares

YIELD: 2 DOZEN

1 cup confectioners' sugar
2 cups unbleached flour
1 cup butter
$^1/_3$ cup honey
$^2/_3$ cup melted unsalted butter

3 tablespoons heavy cream
$^1/_2$ cup packed brown sugar
$3^1/_2$ cups coarsely chopped pecans

SIFT the confectioners' sugar and flour together in a bowl. CUT in 1 cup butter until crumbly. PRESS into a greased 9x13-inch baking pan. BAKE at 350 degrees for 20 minutes. COMBINE the honey, $^2/_3$ cup unsalted butter, cream and brown sugar in a mixer bowl and beat well. STIR in the pecans. SPREAD over the baked layer. CUT into squares.

Cut Shortbread Cookies

YIELD: $2^1/_2$ DOZEN

1 cup butter, softened
$^1/_2$ cup sugar

$2^1/_2$ cups flour

CREAM the butter and sugar in a mixer bowl until light and fluffy. STIR in the flour. MIX the dough using hands. CHILL in the refrigerator. ROLL the dough on a lightly floured surface $^1/_3$ to $^1/_2$ inch thick. CUT into desired shapes. PLACE on ungreased cookie sheets. BAKE at 300 degrees for 20 to 25 minutes or until cookies test done; the cookies will not brown. COOL on a wire rack. DECORATE as desired.

Pressed Shortbread Cookies

YIELD: 2 DOZEN

Raisin Sheet Bar Cookies

YIELD: 6 TO 7 DOZEN

1 cup butter, softened
1/2 cup packed brown sugar

2 cups flour
Food coloring for tinting

CREAM the butter and brown sugar in a mixer bowl until light and fluffy. BEAT in the flour gradually. TINT with food coloring as desired. PRESS through a cookie press fitted with the desired tip. PLACE on ungreased cookie sheets. BAKE at 325 degrees for 10 to 15 minutes or until the cookies test done. DO not brown.

1 cup raisins
1 1/2 cups water
1/2 cup shortening
1 egg
2 cups flour
1 cup sugar
1 teaspoon baking soda
1/2 teaspoon ground nutmeg
1 teaspoon ground cloves

1 teaspoon ground cinnamon
1 teaspoon salt
1/2 cup chopped pecans
2 tablespoons melted butter or
   margarine
2 teaspoons milk
1/2 teaspoon vanilla extract
2 cups sifted confectioners' sugar

COMBINE the raisins, water and shortening in a saucepan. BRING to a boil and reduce the heat. SIMMER for 20 minutes. REMOVE from the heat to cool. PLACE the cooled raisin mixture in a large mixer bowl. ADD the egg, flour, sugar, baking soda, nutmeg, cloves, cinnamon, salt and pecans and mix well. SPREAD in a lightly greased 11x15-inch baking pan. BAKE at 350 degrees for 20 minutes or until a wooden pick inserted in the center comes out clean. COOL in the pan on a wire rack. COMBINE the butter, milk, vanilla and confectioners' sugar in a mixer bowl and beat until smooth. SPREAD over the cooled layer. CUT into 1x2-inch bars.

Fluffy Cranberry Cream Cheese Pie

YIELD: 6 TO 8 SERVINGS

1 1/4 cups cranberry juice cocktail
1 (3-ounce) package raspberry gelatin
1/3 cup sugar
1 cup fresh cranberries, ground
3 ounces cream cheese, softened
1/4 cup sugar
1 tablespoon milk
1 teaspoon vanilla extract
1/2 cup whipping cream
1 (9-inch) baked pie shell, cooled
Whipped cream
Whole cranberries

BRING the cranberry juice to a boil in a saucepan and remove from the heat. COMBINE the gelatin and 1/3 cup sugar in a bowl. ADD the hot cranberry juice, stirring until the sugar and gelatin are dissolved. STIR in the ground cranberries. CHILL until partially set. BEAT the cream cheese, 1/4 cup sugar, milk and vanilla in a mixer bowl until fluffy. BEAT the whipping cream in a mixer bowl until soft peaks form. FOLD into the cream cheese mixture. PLACE the bowl of chilled cranberry mixture in a larger bowl filled with ice water and beat until fluffy. LET stand until the mixture mounds if necessary. LAYER the cream cheese mixture and cranberry mixture in the baked pie shell. GARNISH with additional whipped cream piped around the edge and whole cranberries.

Key Limelight Pie

YIELD: 6 SERVINGS

8 ounces lemon yogurt
1 tablespoon unflavored gelatin
$1/4$ cup cold water
$1/2$ cup sugar
$1/4$ teaspoon salt
$1/2$ cup Key lime juice
$11/2$ teaspoons freshly grated
lime zest
5 drops of green food coloring (optional)
2 egg whites
$1/3$ cup sugar
1 cup lowfat whipped cream
1 (9-inch) graham cracker pie shell
Whipped cream
Lime slices

PLACE a fine sieve lined with cheesecloth over a bowl. ADD the yogurt. STRAIN in the refrigerator for 6 hours or until the whey has separated from the yogurt. SOFTEN the gelatin in the cold water. COMBINE with $1/2$ cup sugar and salt in a saucepan. STIR in the lime juice. BRING to a boil over medium heat. REMOVE from the heat. ADD the yogurt, lime zest and food coloring and mix well. CHILL in the refrigerator until the mixture mounds when dropped from a spoon, stirring occasionally. BEAT the egg whites in a mixer bowl until soft peaks form. ADD $1/3$ cup sugar gradually, beating constantly until stiff peaks form. FOLD into the gelatin mixture. FOLD in the whipped cream. SPOON into the graham cracker crust. CHILL until firm. SERVE with additional whipped cream and garnish with lime slices.

Shoofly Pies

YIELD: 12 SERVINGS

2 cups molasses or corn syrup
1 cup hot water
1 cup packed light brown sugar
1 teaspoon (scant) baking soda
2 tablespoons vinegar
2 (10-inch) unbaked deep-dish
   pie shells

5 cups flour
2 cups packed light brown sugar
$^1/_2$ teaspoon cream of tartar
1 tablespoon ground cinnamon
2 teaspoons ground nutmeg

COMBINE the molasses, hot water, 1 cup brown sugar, baking soda and vine-gar in a bowl. STIR until the brown sugar is dissolved and the mixture is of a syrupy consistency. POUR into the unbaked pie shells. MIX the flour, 2 cups brown sugar, cream of tartar, cinnamon and nutmeg in a bowl until crumbly. SPRINKLE over the top of the pies. BAKE at 450 degrees for 10 minutes. REDUCE the oven temperature to 375 degrees. BAKE for 30 minutes longer. REDUCE the oven temperature to 350 degrees. BAKE for 30 minutes longer.

Chocolate Sauce

YIELD: 8 SERVINGS

1 ounce unsweetened chocolate
1 tablespoon butter
$^1/_3$ cup boiling water
1 cup sugar

2 tablespoons light corn syrup
$^1/_8$ teaspoon salt
1 teaspoon vanilla extract

MELT the chocolate and butter in a saucepan, stirring constantly. STIR in the boiling water. COOK until thickened, stirring constantly. ADD the sugar, corn syrup and salt. COOK for 5 minutes, stirring occasionally. STIR in the vanilla. SERVE immediately.

NOTE: If the sauce begins to turn to sugar, stir in a small amount of cream.

Hot Fudge Sauce

YIELD: 1 CUP

1/2 cup sugar
3 tablespoons Droste or Dutch process
   baking cocoa

1 (8-ounce) can evaporated milk
3 tablespoons butter

COMBINE the sugar, cocoa, evaporated milk and butter in a saucepan. BRING to a boil and reduce the heat. SIMMER until thickened, stirring constantly. SERVE over ice cream.

Fruit Compote Sauce

YIELD: 8 TO 12 SERVINGS

1 (15-ounce) can pears
1 (15-ounce) can dark sweet cherries
1 (20-ounce) can pineapple
1 (16-ounce) can peaches
1 (16-ounce) jar applesauce

3/4 cup packed brown sugar
1/2 cup margarine
Chopped pecans (optional)
Ground cinnamon (optional)
Ground nutmeg (optional)

COMBINE the pears, cherries, pineapple and peaches in a bowl. SPOON into a 9x13-inch baking dish. HEAT the applesauce, brown sugar and margarine in a saucepan until blended, stirring frequently. POUR over the fruit. SPRINKLE with pecans, cinnamon and nutmeg. BAKE at 250 degrees for 20 minutes or until bubbly. SERVE warm.

Whiskey Sauce

YIELD: ABOUT ¾ CUP

½ cup butter   3 tablespoons bourbon
1 cup confectioners' sugar

MELT the butter in a medium saucepan. WHISK in the confectioners' sugar. STIR in the whiskey. SERVE over bread pudding.

NOTE: Can substitute rum or blended whiskey for the bourbon.

Gold Brick Topping

YIELD: ¾ CUP

½ cup butter or margarine   1 bar German's chocolate
½ cup chopped pecans

MELT the butter in a small saucepan. STIR in the pecans. SAUTÉ for 4 to 5 minutes. BREAK the chocolate into pieces and add to the saucepan. HEAT until the chocolate melts, stirring frequently. SERVE over ice cream.

NOTE: The sauce will harden over the ice cream.

Contributors

Lisa Adams
Sherry Wood Aldrin
Kellie Schoedinger Ali
Anna Allen
Natalie Kapral Baur
Pam Bertram
Margaret Black
Sunny Bright
Nancy Brigner
Shirley Acker Britt
Loren Brunemann
Amy Buckles
Melissa Buller
Mary Lynn Buster
Kim Byrd
Donna Vuletic Caldwell
Mary Campbell
Mary Cantwell
Lisa Carlin
Marjorie Mead Carlson
Melinda S. Carlson
Cynthia Chester
Carolyn Claycomb
Ida Copenhaver
Miranda Cox
Julie Cress
Linda Cummins

Jill Darling
Sandy DeCrane
Yvonne Dixon
Mary Dorsey
Nancy Drees
Laura Drobnich
Duncan Hines®
Amy Dunn
Jody Dzuranin
Elizabeth Eberts-Slinger
Beth Eck
Beth Feucht
Carolyn Folk
Susan Fortner
Cecilia Roman Gerling
Elsa C. Giammarco
Mary D. Ginter
Janie Greiner
Mary Gross
Wendy Haddow
Julie Hadley
Kathy Haidet
Janet Halliday
Sue Hallin
Beth Hamilton
Katie Hamilton
Lisa Hays

Patricia Henahan
Amy Jo Hernandez
Rex Ann Hill
Ronda Hobart
Kathy Hoffman
Louise Holland
Pat Howland
Linda Hutaff
Allison Johnson
Constance Jump
Cynthia Karkut
Susan Keferl
Marilyn Kraemer Kiep
Valarie S. Klosz
Sally Chard Kosnik
Suzanne Kull
Therese Lambert
Suzy Leneo
Suzy Lhamon
Suzy Kramer Lucci
Dawn Marable
Patti Mathaus
Jeanne McCoy
Louise McCulloch
Rebecca McNemar
Sally Meier
Judy Mosier

Laura Murphy
Bunny Nolt
Ann Oakley
Mary Beth O'Brien
Renee O'Brien
Patty Offenberg
Clara Owens
Annita Paolucci
Jenifer Peponis
Kelly Peterson
Dawna Petkash-Beckett
Ginger Pettit
Shelia Khosh Phillips
Maria Pidcock
Sue Pinkerton
Nancy Prellwitz
Lauri Prescott
Theresa Diserio Ramsay
Cortney Randall
Nancy Recchie
Jeanne V. Reed
Leslie Stratton Rich
Jennifer Richards
Edna Risell
Sarah Roesch
Marcie Rogell
Jo Ann Rohyans

Liz Ryan
Nancy Sanders
Jean Sankey
Sandy Schirmer
Liddy Schmitz
Lynda Schnedl
Lynda Schockman
Jeanne Schoedinger
Lisa Takos Schoedinger
Janet Schuler
Lynn Schwarz
Julie Depew Shaffer
Carol Sheehan
Pam Shisler
Carey Smith
Stacie Smith
Susan Smith
Bev Soult
Amy Strauss
Sandy Taironen
Catherine Talda
Lee Thornbury
Peggy Tidwell
Rachael Timmons
Gillian Trimmer
Ann Ullom-Morse
Patti Vande Werken

Helen Walker
Clover Ward
Katherine Weislogel
Gail Whitcomb
Betty G. Williams
Celeste Williams
Kristin Williams
Marjorie Yoder
Maryanne Yoder

Index

Accompaniments
American Devonshire Cream, 19
Amish Peach Jam, 135
Brandied Apple Butter, 134
Dried Cherry Chutney, 70
Hoisin Catsup, 67
Honey Mustard, 118
Italian Relish, 119
Kelton House Cranberry Relish, 119
Microwave Pumpkin Butter, 135
Peach Catsup, 118
Rosemary Whipped Cream, 23

Appetizers. *See also* Dips; Salsas;
Spreads
Brie with Sun-Dried Tomatoes, 35
Chive Puffs with Curried Chicken
Filling, 14
Creole Spiced Tortilla Chips, 32
Figgy Bleu Torte, 38
Ham Balls in Sweet-and-Sour
Currant Sauce, 39
Ham Puffs, 40
Italian Crostini, 39
Pesto Torte with Garlic Toasts, 37
Salmon Ball, 38
Shrimp Nachos, 40
Southern Cheese Straws, 41
Spinach and Mushroom
Cheesecake, 36
Sweet Potato Biscuits with Spicy
Turkey Pâté, 17

Apple
Apple Marshmallow Glaze, 24
Brandied Apple Butter, 134
Christmas Fruit Salad Mold, 56
Easy Apple Coffee Cake, 125
Fruit Compote Sauce, 166

Morning Glory Muffins, 132
Okinawa Wassail, 43
Old-Fashioned Oatmeal Pancakes, 126
Rosemary Apple Tea Cakes, 23

Artichoke
Crabmeat-Stuffed Avocados, 49
Pasta and Grilled Chicken Caesar, 94
Shrimp and Artichoke Primavera, 97
Spinach Artichoke Dip, 31

Asparagus
Asparagus Frittata Squares, 15
Chicken, Ham and Asparagus
Lasagna, 93

Avocado
Chicken Salad Northwoods, 48
Crabmeat-Stuffed Avocados, 49

Banana
Banana Cake with Caramel
Frosting, 144
Bananas Foster, 138
Banana Split Bread, 130

Beef. *See also* Ground Beef
Beef Tenderloin with Médoc
Sauce, 64
Grilled London Broil with Red Wine
Marinade, 65
Marinated Steak Salad, 46
Spicy Marinated Flank Steak, 65
Spicy Sesame Teriyaki Shish
Kabobs, 66

Beverages
Chocolate Mocha Punch, 42
Doc's Bloody Marys, 41

Okinawa Wassail, 43
Peach Sangria, 42
Winter's Treat Hot Buttered Rum
Mix, 43

Biscotti
Anise Biscotti, 156
Orange and Cinnamon Biscotti, 157

Biscuits
Chili Pecan Biscuits, 127
Sweet Potato Biscuits, 17

Black Beans
Black Bean Hummus, 31
Black Bean Pâté, 34
Black Bean Soup, 59

Breads. *See also* Biscuits; Muffins;
Pancakes; Rolls; Scones
Apricot Nut Bread, 130
Banana Split Bread, 130
Blueberry Sour Cream Tea
Ring, 125
Cheese Popovers, 134
Cranberry Bread, 131
Easy Apple Coffee Cake, 125
Garlic Toasts, 37
Honey White Bread, 129
Peanut Butter Bread with Strawberry
Butter, 131

Broccoli
Broccoli and Shrimp Stir-Fry, 86
Broccoli Mops with Ginger Sauce, 106
Italian Pasta Salad, 55
Pasta with Broccoli and Goat
Cheese, 101
Sesame Broccoli Salad, 50

Cakes

Almond Cake with Raspberry
Sauce, 143
Banana Cake with Caramel
Frosting, 144
Cappuccino Bonbons, 154
Carrot Layer Cake, 145
Chocolate Mousse Torte, 150
Double Chocolate Cake with
Chocolate Ganache, 146
Gingerbread, 154
Ginger Pound Cake, 24
Holiday Eggnog Cake, 153
Milky Way Cake, 147
Miniature Amaretto Fruitcakes, 25
Mocha Chocolate Torte, 152
Red Velvet Cake with Mock Whipped
Frosting, 149
Rosemary Apple Tea Cakes, 23
Sour Cream Chocolate Cake with Sour
Cream Chocolate Frosting, 148

Candy

Molded Cream Cheese Mints, 27
Square Buckeyes, 155
Sweet Clouds, 156
White Chocolate Brittle, 155

Carrot

Carrot Layer Cake, 145
Carrot Soup, 60
Horseradish Carrots, 107
Morning Glory Muffins, 132
Orange-Glazed Carrots, 107
Potato and Carrot Pudding, 111

Catsup

Hoisin Catsup, 67
Peach Catsup, 118

Cheesecakes

Fudge Truffle Cheesecake, 138
Miniature Chocolate Cheesecakes, 20
Miniature Lavender Cheesecakes, 21
Pumpkin Cheesecake with Maple
Pecan Glaze, 139
Spinach and Mushroom
Cheesecake, 36
Welsh Cheesecakes, 20

Chicken

Baked Apricot Chicken, 74
Chicken and Smoked Almond Tea
Sandwiches, 13
Chicken Chimichangas, 81
Chicken Elizabeth, 78
Chicken, Ham and Asparagus
Lasagna, 93
Chicken Salad Northwoods, 48
Chicken with Honey, 80
Chive Puffs with Curried Chicken
Filling, 14
Cranberry Chicken, 75
Creamy Almond Chicken, 74
Fiesta Chicken Salad, 47
Grilled Chicken Breasts with Orange
Mint Pesto, 79
Grilled Plum Chicken, 80
Hawaiian Chicken, 75
Kelton House Chicken Divan, 76
Lemon Chicken, 77
Mexican Chicken, 77
Pasta and Grilled Chicken Caesar, 94
Pecan and Peanut Chicken Breasts
with Pesto Sauce, 79
Pecan Chicken, 78
Pollo Tonnato, 82
Spicy Sesame Teriyaki Shish
Kabobs, 66

Chocolate

Cappuccino Bonbons, 154
Chocolate Cranberry Cookies, 158
Chocolate Ganache, 146
Chocolate Glaze, 151
Chocolate Mint Squares, 159
Chocolate Mocha Punch, 42
Chocolate Mousse, 151
Chocolate Mousse Torte, 150
Chocolate Sauce, 165
Double Chocolate Cake with
Chocolate Ganache, 146
Fresh Fruit Fool in Chocolate Cups, 21
Fudge Truffle Cheesecake, 138
Gold Brick Topping, 167
Hot Fudge Sauce, 166
Milky Way Cake, 147
Milky Way Icing, 147
Miniature Chocolate Cheesecakes, 20
Mocha Chocolate Torte, 152
Sour Cream Chocolate Cake with Sour
Cream Chocolate Frosting, 148
Square Buckeyes, 155
White Chocolate Brittle, 155
White Chocolate Brownies, 158
White Chocolate Mousse and Berry
Trifle, 22

Cookies

Anise Biscotti, 156
Chocolate Cranberry Cookies, 158
Chocolate Mint Squares, 159
Cut Shortbread Cookies, 161
Old-Fashioned Lemon Bars, 160
Orange and Cinnamon Biscotti, 157
Pecan Squares, 161
Pressed Shortbread Cookies, 162
Raisin Sheet Bar Cookies, 162
White Chocolate Brownies, 158

Crabmeat
Crabmeat Cakes, 85
Crabmeat-Stuffed Avocados, 49
Seafood Lasagna, 99
Watercress and Crabmeat Quiche, 16

Cranberry
Chocolate Cranberry Cookies, 158
Christmas Fruit Salad Mold, 56
Cranberry Bread, 131
Cranberry Chicken, 75
Cranberry Congealed Salad, 56
Fluffy Cranberry Cream Cheese
    Pie, 163
Kelton House Cranberry Relish, 119

Creams
American Devonshire Cream, 19
Rosemary Whipped Cream, 23

Cucumber
Cucumber and Mint Tea
    Sandwiches, 10
Kelton House Gazpacho, 58
Shrimp and Cucumber Tea
    Sandwiches, 15
White Gazpacho, 58

Desserts. *See also* Cakes; Candy;
    Cheesecakes; Cookies; Pies
Bananas Foster, 138
Caramel Soufflé, 140
Espresso Ice, 142
Fresh Fruit Fool in Chocolate Cups, 21
Fudge Truffle Cheesecake, 138
Lime Fool with Strawberries and
    Kiwifruit, 141
Pumpkin Cheesecake with Maple
    Pecan Glaze, 139

Vodka and Grapefruit Sorbet, 142
White Chocolate Mousse and Berry
    Trifle, 22

Desserts, Sauces
Chocolate Sauce, 165
Fruit Compote Sauce, 166
Gold Brick Topping, 167
Hot Fudge Sauce, 166
Raspberry Sauce, 143
Whiskey Sauce, 167

Dips
Black Bean Hummus, 31
Parmesan Pesto Dip, 30
Skyline® Chili Dip, 30
Spinach Artichoke Dip, 31

Egg Dishes. *See also* Quiches
Asparagus Frittata Squares, 15
Cheese Fondue Casserole, 122
Egg and Watercress Tea
    Sandwiches, 11
Ham and Cheese Picnic Pie, 72
Night-Before French Toast
    Casserole, 126
Savory Breakfast Casserole, 122
Zesty Brunch Enchiladas, 123

Fig
Figgy Bleu Torte, 38

Fish. *See also* Salmon; Tuna
Grilled Grouper, 83
Herb and Garlic Fish, 83

Frostings
Buttercream Frosting, 128
Caramel Frosting, 144

Chocolate Ganache, 146
Cream Cheese Frosting, 145
Creamy Frosting, 160
Eggnog Fluff, 153
Milky Way Icing, 147
Mock Whipped Frosting, 149
Sour Cream Chocolate
    Frosting, 148

Gazpacho
Kelton House Gazpacho, 58
White Gazpacho, 58

Glazes
Apple Marshmallow Glaze, 24
Chocolate Glaze, 151
Maple Pecan Glaze, 139

Ground Beef
Teriyaki Hamburgers, 67

Ham
Chicken Elizabeth, 78
Chicken, Ham and Asparagus
    Lasagna, 93
Ham and Cheese Picnic Pie, 72
Ham Balls in Sweet-and-Sour Currant
    Sauce, 39
Ham Puffs, 40
Minced Ham and Pineapple Tea
    Sandwiches with Honey Butter, 13
Zesty Brunch Enchiladas, 123

Jam
Amish Peach Jam, 135

Jicama
Green Salad with Jicama and
    Orange Poppy Seed Dressing, 53

Lamb
Greek Lamb Shanks, 73
Grilled Garlic Lamb Chops, 73
Spicy Sesame Teriyaki Shish
    Kabobs, 66

Lasagna
Chicken, Ham and Asparagus
    Lasagna, 93
Sausage and Pepperoni
    Lasagna, 90
Seafood Lasagna, 99

Lavender
Lavender Sugar, 19
Lavender Sugar Scones, 19
Miniature Lavender Cheesecakes, 21

Lemon
Lemon Chicken, 77
Lemon Macaroon Tarts, 26
Lemon Rice, 116
Old-Fashioned Lemon Bars, 160
Sweet Lemon Cream Scones, 18

Menus
An Afternoon Invitation, 9
A Special Gathering, 89
A Work of Art, 29
Blue Ribbon Brunch, 121
Enchanted Evenings, 63
Let's Do Lunch, 45
Sweet Dreams, 137
The Game Plan, 105

Muffins
Date and Oatmeal Yogurt
    Muffins, 132
Morning Glory Muffins, 132

Pineapple Muffins, 133
Pumpkin Muffins, 133

Orange
Cranberry Congealed Salad, 56
Green Salad with Jicama, 53
Grilled Chicken Breasts with Orange
    Mint Pesto, 79
Orange and Cinnamon Biscotti, 157
Orange-Glazed Carrots, 107
Orange Poppy Seed Dressing, 53

Pancakes
Finnish Pancake, 127
Old-Fashioned Oatmeal Pancakes, 126

Pasta. *See also* Lasagna; Salads, Pasta
Greek-Style Shrimp with Pasta, 98
Layered Pasta Ricotta Pie, 100
Linguini with Sun-Dried Tomato
    Pesto, 102
Linguini with Tomato and Basil
    Sauce, 102
Mom's Best Manicotti, 91
Mushroom Saffron Sauce over
    Fettuccini, 101
Pasta and Grilled Chicken Caesar, 94
Pasta with Broccoli and Goat
    Cheese, 101
Pasta with Shrimp and Feta, 98
Pasta with Spicy Tomato Cream
    Sauce, 103
Pasta with Tuna Sauce, 94
Rigatoni in a Woodsman's Sauce, 92
Salmon Tetrazzini, 95
Shrimp and Artichoke Primavera, 97
Shrimp Fettuccini, 97
Spaghetti with Scallops, Roasted Red
    Peppers and Pine Nuts, 96

Spicy Valentine Fettuccini, 90
Tortellini with Smoked Salmon and
    Dill, 95

Peach
Amish Peach Jam, 135
Fruit Compote Sauce, 166
Peach Catsup, 118
Peach Sangria, 42

Pesto
Basil Pesto, 12
Parmesan Pesto Dip, 30
Pecan and Peanut Chicken Breasts
    with Pesto Sauce, 79
Pesto Torte with Garlic Toasts, 37
Sun-Dried Tomato Pesto, 12

Pie Pastries
Macaroon Tart Shells, 26

Pies. *See also* Tarts
Fluffy Cranberry Cream Cheese
    Pie, 163
Key Limelight Pie, 164
Shoofly Pies, 165

Pork. *See also* Ham; Sausage
Embers Pork Chops, 71
Fiesta Pork, 68
Grilled Spiced Pork Tenderloins with
    Dried Cherry Chutney, 70
Ham Balls in Sweet-and-Sour Currant
    Sauce, 39
Jamaican Pork Tenderloin, 68
Medallions of Pork with
    Prunes, 69
Mom's Best Manicotti, 91
Rice Delmonico, 115

Potato
Bleu Cheese and Bacon Potatoes, 111
Mashed Red Potatoes, 112
Potato and Carrot Pudding, 111
Tarragon Potato Salad, 51

Poultry. *See* Chicken; Turkey

Pumpkin
Microwave Pumpkin Butter, 135
Pumpkin Cheesecake with Maple
   Pecan Glaze, 139
Pumpkin Muffins, 133

Quiches
Gruyère and Shallot Quiches, 123
Salmon Quiche, 124
Watercress and Crabmeat Quiche, 16

Relish
Italian Relish, 119
Kelton House Cranberry
   Relish, 119

Rice
Curried Shrimp and Wild Rice, 87
Garlic Rice, 116
Lemon Rice, 116
Microwave Risotto, 117
Rice Delmonico, 115
Rice with Mushrooms and
   Onions, 117

Rolls
Cinnamon Rolls, 128
Herbed Spoon Rolls, 129

Salad Dressings
Dijon Vinaigrette, 48

Mustard Vinaigrette, 46
Orange Poppy Seed Dressing, 53
Poppy Seed Dressing, 54
Spanish Salad Dressing, 54
Sweet and Tangy Mustard
   Dressing, 52

Salads
Chicken Salad Northwoods, 48
Crabmeat-Stuffed Avocados, 49
Curried Tuna Salad, 50
Fiesta Chicken Salad, 47
Green Salad with Jicama and Orange
   Poppy Seed Dressing, 53
Marinated Steak Salad, 46
Romaine Salad with Sweet and Tangy
   Mustard Dressing, 52
Sesame Broccoli Salad, 50
Strawberry Spinach Salad with Poppy
   Seed Dressing, 54
Tarragon Potato Salad, 51
Tomato Bread Salad, 51

Salads, Fruit
Christmas Fruit Salad Mold, 56
Cranberry Congealed Salad, 56

Salads, Pasta
Italian Pasta Salad, 55
Mediterranean Pasta Salad, 55

Salmon
Grilled Salmon Steaks with Sun-Dried
   Tomato Sauce, 84
Salmon Ball, 38
Salmon Quiche, 124
Salmon Tetrazzini, 95
Spicy Sesame Teriyaki Shish
   Kabobs, 66

Tortellini with Smoked Salmon and
   Dill, 95

Salsas
Black-Eyed Pea Salsa, 33
Gazpacho Salsa with Creole Spiced
   Tortilla Chips, 32
Summer Salsa, 33

Sandwiches
Chèvre and Herb Butter Tea
   Sandwiches, 10
Chicken and Smoked Almond Tea
   Sandwiches, 13
Cucumber and Mint Tea
   Sandwiches, 10
Curried Chicken Filling, 14
Egg and Watercress Tea
   Sandwiches, 11
Minced Ham and Pineapple Tea
   Sandwiches with Honey
   Butter, 13
Onion Tea Sandwiches, 11
Pesto Ribbon Tea Sandwiches, 12
Shrimp and Cucumber Tea
   Sandwiches, 15

Sauces
Cheddar Cheese Sauce, 49
Marinara Sauce, 103
Médoc Sauce, 64
Red Sauce, 71
Sesame Teriyaki Glaze, 66

Sausage
Rigatoni in a Woodsman's Sauce, 92
Sausage and Pepperoni Lasagna, 90
Savory Breakfast Casserole, 122
Spicy Valentine Fettuccini, 90

Scallops
Seafood Lasagna, 99
Spaghetti with Scallops, Roasted Red
Peppers and Pine Nuts, 96

Scones
Coconut Scones, 18
Lavender Sugar Scones, 19
Sweet Lemon Cream Scones, 18

Shellfish. *See* Crabmeat; Scallops;
Shrimp

Shrimp
Broccoli and Shrimp Stir-Fry, 86
Cashew Shrimp, 85
Curried Shrimp and Wild Rice, 87
Greek-Style Shrimp with
Pasta, 98
Marinated Shrimp, 87
Pasta with Shrimp and Feta, 98
Seafood Lasagna, 99
Shrimp and Artichoke Primavera, 97
Shrimp and Cucumber Tea
Sandwiches, 15
Shrimp Fettuccini, 97
Shrimp Nachos, 40

Side Dishes. *See also* Accompaniments
Garlic Rice, 116
Lemon Rice, 116
Microwave Risotto, 117
Rice Delmonico, 115
Rice with Mushrooms and
Onions, 117
Sun-Dried Tomato Polenta
Gratin, 115

Soups, Cold
Kelton House Gazpacho, 58
Spinach Mint Soup, 57
Strawberry Soup, 57
White Gazpacho, 58

Soups, Hot
Black Bean Soup, 59
Carrot Soup, 60
Cream of Chestnut Soup, 61
Lentil Chili, 61
Spinach Mint Soup, 57
Vermont Cheddar Soup, 60

Spinach
Layered Pasta Ricotta
Pie, 100
Savory Breakfast Casserole, 122
Spinach and Mushroom
Cheesecake, 36
Spinach Artichoke Dip, 31
Spinach Delight, 113
Spinach Mint Soup, 57
Strawberry Spinach Salad with Poppy
Seed Dressing, 54

Spreads
Black Bean Pâté, 34
Islander Cheese Spread, 35
Rumaki Pâté, 34

Strawberry
Lime Fool with Strawberries and
Kiwifruit, 141
Peach Sangria, 42
Peanut Butter Bread with Strawberry
Butter, 131

Strawberry Soup, 57
Strawberry Spinach Salad with Poppy
Seed Dressing, 54
White Chocolate Mousse and Berry
Trifle, 22

Tarts
Butter Tarts, 27
Lemon Macaroon Tarts, 26

Tuna
Curried Tuna Salad, 50
Pasta with Tuna Sauce, 94
Pollo Tonnato, 82

Turkey
Lentil Chili, 61
Sweet Potato Biscuits with Spicy
Turkey Pâté, 17

Vegetables. *See also* Individual Kinds
Barbecued Green Beans, 108
Corn Pudding, 108
Good-For-You Refried Beans, 109
Green Beans Provençal, 109
Mushrooms in Wine Sauce, 110
Roasted Red Bell Peppers, 112
Roasted Rosemary Vegetables, 114
Sautéed Peas with Walnuts, 110
Southern Yam Bake, 114
Tomato Pie, 113

Watercress
Egg and Watercress Tea
Sandwiches, 11
Watercress and Crabmeat
Quiche, 16

Order Information

For information on ordering additional copies of
America Celebrates Columbus, contact:

The Junior League of Columbus, Inc.
Attention: Cookbook
The English House
583 Franklin Avenue
Columbus, Ohio 43215-4715
Telephone: (614) 470-2955
Fax: (614) 464-2718

Proceeds from the sale of *America Celebrates Columbus* are returned to the
community through the projects of the Junior League of Columbus.